# THE MASTER AND THE DISCIPLE

## SRI CHINMOY

# TABLE OF CONTENTS

# THE MASTER AND THE DISCIPLE

## SRI CHINMOY

Library of Congress card catalog no. 85-072172

ISBN: 0-88497-884-3

Printed by: Agni Press, 84-47 Parsons Blvd.
Jamaica, N.Y. 11432

# INTRODUCTION

What is a genuine spiritual Master, and what kind of wisdom does he embody? Who are his disciples and what force compels them to follow him? In this remarkable collection of writings, spiritual Master Sri Chinmoy illumines for us the deeply moving dynamic that binds the spiritual Master or Guru and his disciple. This dynamic is eloquent with love, and testifies to a transforming vision of life. Sri Chinmoy's words reveal a higher spiritual truth whose pursuit is charted by the odyssey that spiritual Master and disciple undertake together. The nature of that odyssey deserves our understanding.

In Sri Chinmoy's terms, a true spiritual Master or Guru is someone who has attained God-realisation, ultimate perfection in the wisdom of life, and who seeks to convey this wisdom to others. To anyone with an ardent hunger for inner knowledge and peace, such wisdom is readily visible in the God-realised soul. Sri Chinmoy himself emanates a radiance and peace so profound, and a love so accepting and unconditional, that one cannot escape feeling a quiet delight in his presence. The illumined Master conveys his wisdom seldom by words and never by didactic instruction. His teaching is the silence of his gaze, the harmony of his gestures, the compassion of his smile and the infinitude of his heart. His authority stems from his love and peace, and it is for the sake of these that the disciple binds himself with willing devotion to his Master's will.

There are few God-realised souls and still fewer God-realised spiritual Masters. As Sri Chinmoy points out, the genuine spiritual Master, recognising that the inner wealth he has discovered is each man's birthright and hidden treasure, offers his gift to suffering and seeking individuals everywhere. This gift of necessity comes without charge, for love and peace have no price and teach us to see their reflection in all created things. And so, with infinite compassion, the spiritual Master takes frustration and pain from those who come to him and gives in return his own peace and joy.

A spiritual Master is an artist of infinite patience. In him are joined the determination of a dauntless warrior and the gentleness of the tenderest mother. Using years as his time frame, he sculpts the recalcitrant human material of his disciples into the very image of peace. This task is enormous. For peace is as natural to the soul of man as air is to breathing, yet peace evades us. Each of us claims to want nothing more than peace, yet each of us lives in a sea of turbulence. The fault lies in our own ignorance, doubt and inadequate devotion to the source of peace within us. And so the spiritual Master must repeatedly compel his disciples to turn away from false solutions to the aggravations of life and to find their own ultimate refuge in the shrine of their hearts.

Through his own childlike simplicity, joy and serenity, the Master continually offers the disciple an image of the disciple's own true goal. At first the Master's influence provides the disciple with repeated but temporary experiences of tranquility and delight. But over time these experiences generate in the disciple a budding faith in his own inner potential. This faith hungers for the realisation of its own inner vision. Sri

Chinmoy writes, "It is the spiritual Master's job to make his disciples feel that without love, without truth and light, life is meaningless and fruitless. The most important thing a spiritual Master does for his spiritual children is to make them consciously aware of something vast and infinite within themselves, which is nothing other than God Himself."

For Sri Chinmoy, the principal vehicle of spiritual instruction is meditation, through which the Master gradually brings forward qualities which will enable the disciple to make inner progress and to counteract the pull of self-destructive and negative forces and habits. Through meditation, the disciple begins a process which eventually transforms the roots of his being. This process compels him to cease identifying himself with outer events, the successes and failures of his life. Instead, he begins to find an unfaltering source within himself, a source so profound that it is unperturbed by the vicissitudes of life. Each event in life, whether joyful or painful, becomes an occasion through which the disciple deepens his devotion to this source of remarkable beauty, and cherishes the delight it offers him. The mysterious journey towards this unknown source unfolds in a miracle of joy and gratitude which, for the true seeker, becomes the compelling reality of his life. All other experiences lose importance against the necessity of this journey towards peace, light and delight.

Sri Chinmoy tells us that as the spiritual Master fosters his cherished disciples' inner hunger, he leads them to recognise that his height and his realisation of infinite Peace are their own. When the disciple feels this truth, he understands that true obedience to his Master is nothing other than his constant determination to remain in his heart and to claim his Master's light for himself. Outer obedience, or compliance with the spiritual Guru's advice and requests, only expresses the inner recognition that just because his Master is all for him, the disciple longs to be all for his Master. Because he is one with his Master, the disciple makes his Master's vision his own. Because the Master is one with his disciple, he gladly accepts the disciple's imperfections as his own, and takes full responsibility for transforming those imperfections into perfections.

With wondering gratitude, the disciple sees again and again that his own self-love, fraught with self-doubt, is nothing compared to the love his Master cherishes for him. At first hesitantly, and then with increasing devotion, he abandons himself to the experience of this love. With the healing power of his compassion the Master slowly replaces his disciple's limitations with sincerity of mind, purity of heart and devotion to a sacred vision of life.

Sri Chinmoy calls his path a path of love, devotion and surrender. The disciple loves his Master, and through him loves his own higher self. He devotes himself to the nourishment, with infinite care and tender affection, of the reality his Master brings forth within him. And finally, he gladly surrenders his whole being, with all its imperfections, to the will of his own reality. Through his oneness with his Guru, he learns that each of us possesses God within himself, and that all of creation is nothing but God's Light. He sees that his role is simply to be of this Light, to manifest it and to love and cherish it in others. With a flood of delight, he embraces the gift of life. With gratitude, he offers this life to his Master's vision. And with unfathomable compassion, his Master shows him his own life's ocean of peace.

*Sunanda*

*PROLOGUE*

## THE GURU

The Guru sees in his disciple the very image of God; so he is all sacrifice to the disciple. The disciple sees and feels in his Guru the only shelter of his limitations; so he is all love for his Guru.

The Guru's love for his disciple is his strength. The disciple's surrender towards his Guru is the disciple's strength.

The Guru is at once the source of the disciple's achievements and a most faithful servant of the disciple's love.

The Guru has only one compassionate weapon: forgiveness. The disciple has three naked swords: limitation, weakness and ignorance. Nevertheless, the Guru wins with great ease.

To achieve realisation by oneself alone is like crossing the ocean in a raft. But to achieve realisation through the grace of a Guru is like crossing the ocean in a swift and strong boat, which ferries you safely across the sea of ignorance to the Golden Shore.

O disciple, do you know the most foolish customer on earth? He is your Guru and your Guru alone. He buys your ignorance and gives you knowledge; he buys your impotence and gives you power. Can you ever imagine a more foolish bargain? Now learn the name of your Guru's foolishness: compassion and nothing else.

## *YOUR REAL TEACHER*

He who inspires you
    Is your real teacher.

He who loves you
    Is your real teacher.

He who forces you
    Is your real teacher.

He who perfects you
    Is your real teacher.

He who treasures you
    Is your real teacher.

# 1

# The Role of
# the Guru

The human teacher shows you
  How to read.
The teacher divine sleeplessly
  Reads for you.
The one leads your mind
  To wisdom's portal,
The other opens your soul
  To the sky-vast Blue.

## THE ROLE OF THE GURU

A real spiritual Master is one who has attained God-realisation. Everyone is one with God, but the real spiritual Master has established his conscious oneness with God. At any moment he can enter into a higher consciousness and bring down messages from God to those disciples who have faith in him. The Master, if he is genuine, represents God on earth for those seekers who have real aspiration and faith in him. He has been authorised or commissioned by God to help them. The real Teacher, the real Guru, is God Himself. But on earth He will often operate in and through a spiritual Master. The Master energises the seeker with inspiration and, in the course of time, through the infinite Grace of the Supreme, offers the seeker illumination.

You make a mistake when you take the Master as only a person, as the human body. You have to feel that the real Master is inside the physical. Why have my disciples come to me? It is because their real Master, the Supreme, is inside me. The Supreme is also inside them, but in them He is still sleeping whereas in me He is fully awake. The Master and the disciple are like two friends who have the same capacity, but one is sleeping and needs help in getting up before he can manifest his capacity. The Guru is somebody who will come and touch his brother's feet and caress his head and say, "Please get up. It is time for us to work for our Father."

When a Master accepts someone as a disciple, he accepts that person as part of himself. If the disciple is imperfect, then the Master also remains imperfect. In the disciple's perfection lies the Master's perfection. I always say that I have no individuality, no personality. It is my disciples' achievements that will take me either to Heaven or to hell. I have the capacity to remain all the time in Heaven, but they can easily drag me to hell at every moment because I have accepted them as my own.

A real spiritual Master tries to bring to the fore the inner divinity of the disciple from deep within the disciple's heart. He knocks at the disciple's heart-door and awakens the divine child in him, which we call the soul. He tells the soul, "You will look after the other members of the family—the physical, the mind and the vital—and take care of them. They are making mistakes constantly. Now give them new life, new meaning, new purpose."

It is the spiritual Master's job to make his disciples feel that without love, without truth and light, life is meaningless and fruitless. The most important thing a spiritual Master does for his spiritual children is to make them consciously aware of something vast and infinite within themselves, which is nothing other than God Himself.

The highest transcendental Truth is within our hearts, but unfortunately we have not yet discovered it. So I ask my disciples to go deep within and meditate on the heart, which houses the soul. Eventually they learn how to contact the soul and start listening to its dictates. At that time they have begun to make real progress toward discovering their highest and deepest Self.

If one is already developed, that is to say, if one has been practising the spiritual life in previous incarnations and is in a position to listen to the dictates of his own inner being, it is not absolutely necessary for him to have a spiritual Master. In that case he has only to go deep within and practise the spiritual life most sincerely. Since he doesn't want a Master's help, he has to depend entirely on himself and on the boundless Grace of God. But we have to know that the spiritual path is very arduous; only on rare occasions have people realised God without the help of a spiritual Master. Most spiritual Masters themselves took help from someone for a day or a month or a year or ten years before they realised God.

As we need teachers for our outer knowledge—to illumine our outer being—so also we need a spiritual Master to help and guide us in our inner life, especially in the beginning. Otherwise, our progress will be very slow and uncertain, and we may become terribly confused. We will get high, elevating experiences, but we will not give them adequate significance. Doubt may eclipse our mind and we will say, "I am just an ordinary person, so how can I have this kind of experience? Perhaps I am deluding myself." Or we will tell our friends, and they will say, "It is all mental hallucination. Forget about the spiritual life." But if there is someone who knows what the Reality is, he will say, "Don't act like a fool. The experiences which you have had are absolutely real." The Master will encourage and inspire the seeker and give him the proper explanations of his experiences. Again, if the seeker is doing something wrong in his meditation, the Master will be in a position to correct him.

Why does one go to the university when one can study at home? It is because he feels that he will get expert instruction from people who know the subject well. Now you know that there have been a few—very, very few—real men of knowledge who did not go to any university. Yes, there are exceptions. Every rule admits of exceptions. God is in everybody, and if a seeker feels that he does not need human help, he is most welcome to try his capacity alone. But if someone is wise and wants to run toward his Goal, instead of stumbling or merely walking, then certainly the help of a Guru can be considerable.

Let us say that I am in London. I know that New York exists and that I have to go back there. What do I need to get me there? An airplane and a pilot. In spite of the fact that I know that New York exists, I cannot get there alone. Similarly, you know that God exists. You want to reach God, but someone has to take you there. As the airplane takes me to New York, someone has to carry you to the Consciousness of God which is deep within you. Someone has to show you how to enter into your own divinity, which is God.

A spiritual Master comes to you with a boat. He says, "Come! If you want to go to the Golden Shore, I will take you. Moreover, once you get into my boat, you can sing in the boat, you can dance, you can even sleep; but I will bring you safely to the Goal."

For millennia we have been swimming in the sea of ignorance. When we become awakened, we want to swim across that sea into the ocean of Light and Delight. If we know that there is a boatman, and that there is a boat which can safely carry us to our goal, then naturally we will try to get help from him. A genuine spiritual Master knows the way and is bound to help us reach the goal. Like a boatman, he will carry us to the other shore.

If anybody helps you in the outer world — a lawyer or a doctor, for example — he will charge you something. But when the Guru takes you to your goal, he will not take anything for himself. You don't have to give even an iota of your wealth to the Guru because he has his own infinite wealth. Eventually you will see that it is all the same wealth. His goal, your goal, everybody's goal is the same: infinite Peace, Light and Bliss. The spiritual Master says, "You are hungry. I have an infinite supply of the divine food that you want, so I don't have to take any of yours."

In human life, if people see that someone has taken help, then they may say, "Oh, he could not do it alone." But a person who is really hungry for God will say, "No matter who offers the food, I am hungry and I want to eat immediately. This is the food that I have been crying for all my life and he is supplying me with it. As long as he is feeding true Divinity to me, let me eat."

If you feel that by accepting a Master you are avoiding your own responsibilities, you are making a mistake. For at that time you are separating yourself from your Master. Those who are my very devoted disciples do not feel that they are strangers. They feel their oneness with me. They feel that I have more capacity than they do, so they identify their little capacity with my greater capacity. When they enter into my capacity, they feel that it is their own capacity that they are entering into, for inside me they see all love and concern.

It is only by feeling your oneness with your Master that you can make real progress. If you feel that you are a stranger or an intruder in your Master's heart, or even if you think that you are just a guest, then you will never succeed in your spiritual life. How long can you stay at your friend's place as a guest? A few days or a month, and then you will have to go away. Even if you feel that you are coming as a friend, still you may go away. But if you feel that his house is your house, then you are safe, eternally safe.

When the disciple and the Master find themselves safe in one another's heart, the hour of initiation is fast approaching. When the Master initiates someone, he gives that person a portion of his life-breath. At the time of initiation, the Guru makes a solemn promise to the individual seeker and to the Supreme

that he will do his best to help the seeker in his
spiritual life, that he will offer his heart and soul to
take the disciple into the highest region of the Beyond.
The Master says to the Supreme, "Unless and until I
have brought this child to You, I shall not leave him;
my game shall not be over." And to the disciple he
says, "From now on, you can count on me; you can
think of me as your own."

At the time of initiation, the Master actually takes
on the disciple's teeming imperfections, both from the
present incarnation and from past incarnations. Of
course, there are real and sincere spiritual Masters as
well as false Masters. Here I am speaking about the
true Masters. Some Masters who are very sincere only
initiate one disciple a month. After they initiate the
disciple they fall sick and suffer terribly, because they
have actually taken on the disciple's imperfections.
Again, there are some spiritual Masters who are able
to initiate many disciples without suffering, because
they have the capacity to throw the imperfections they
take on into the Universal Consciousness. But again,
there are some false Masters who initiate fifty, sixty or
a hundred disciples at a time, or who initiate by
proxy. But this kind of mass initiation is an absurd
deception.

The Guru can initiate the disciple in various ways.
He can perform the initiation in India's traditional
way, while the disciple is meditating. He can also
initiate while the disciple is sleeping or when the disciple is in his normal consciousness, but calm and
quiet. The Guru can initiate the disciple through the
eyes alone. He will look at the disciple, and immediately the person will be initiated—but nobody will
know. A Master can also perform a physical initiation, which is to press the head or the heart or any
part of the body of the disciple. At this time, he tries
to make the physical consciousness feel that initiation

has taken place. But along with this physical action, the Guru will initiate the disciple in a psychic way. At that time the Guru sees and feels the soul of the disciple and acts upon the soul. Initiation can also be done by occult processes or in a dream. If there is no spiritual Master available at the time, God Himself can take a very luminous human form in your dream or during your meditation and can initiate you Himself. But this is very rare. Most of the time initiation is done by a Master.

My disciples do not need to ask me to initiate them outwardly, because I know what is best for them; that is to say, I know whether or not the outer initiation will expedite their inner progress. Very often I initiate my disciples through my third eye, which I feel is the most convincing and effective way. Many have observed my eyes when I am in my highest consciousness. At that time my ordinary eyes, my human eyes, become totally one with my third eye. These two ordinary eyes then receive infinite Light from the third eye, and this Light from my divinely radiating eyes enters into the aspirant's eyes. Immediately the Light enters into the aspirant's whole body and percolates there from head to foot. Then I see the Light, my own Light, the Light of the Supreme, glowing in the disciple's ignorance, and that ignorance offers its gratitude. It says, "Now that I have become yours, now that you have made me yours, I shall be yours forever." At that time I become responsible for illumining the disciple's ignorance, and the disciple becomes responsible for helping me manifest the Supreme on earth.

Just because I have initiated you does not mean that you can go out and initiate somebody else. It is not as if I have told you a Truth and now you can tell it to somebody else. Very often I hear that a Master has initiated someone, and then the disciple goes on initiating somebody else, and then that person goes

on to still another person—like family descendants.
But this kind of initiation has no value. True initiation always has to be done by a God-realised Master;
it cannot be done by proxy. If a Master has the spiritual power to initiate a disciple directly on the occult
plane, that is all right. But if he says he can initiate
someone through a disciple who is still a beginner,
that kind of initiation is absurd. When you see people
in the United States who say they have been asked to
initiate others by their spiritual Master in India, then
rest assured that this is no initiation at all; it is only
deception. Initiation has to be done directly by the
Master, either on the physical plane or in the inner
planes.

When the Guru initiates a disciple, he accepts the
disciple unreservedly and unconditionally. Even if the
disciple goes away after initiation, finding fault with
the Guru, the Guru will act in and through that disciple forever. The disciple may even go to some other
Guru, but the Guru who has initiated him will always
help that particular seeker in the inner world. And if
the new Guru is noble enough, then he will allow the
original Guru to act in and through the disciple. Although the physical connection with the original Guru
is cut off, and physically the Guru is not seeing the
disciple, spiritually he is bound to help him because
he has made a promise to the Supreme.

Even if the disciple does not go to any other Guru
but simply falls from the path of Truth, still his original Guru has to keep his promise. The disciple may
drop from the spiritual path for one incarnation, two
incarnations or even many incarnations, but his Guru—
whether he be in the body or in the higher regions—
will constantly watch over the disciple and wait for
the opportunity to help him actively when he again
turns to the spiritual path. The Guru is truly detached,
but just because he made a promise to the disciple

and to the Supreme in the disciple, the Guru waits indefinitely for an opportunity to take the disciple to the Goal.

Some of my disciples who at one time followed my path most sincerely have also left me most sincerely. But if they are my disciples in the inner world, if I had already accepted them and they were my real disciples, then I wish to say that I have not forgotten them. They may take one, two, five or six incarnations to come back to the life of aspiration, but no matter how long they take, I shall help them in their march towards God-realisation.

Because of the promise I made to the disciple's soul and to God, I am more responsible for each disciple than the disciple himself. But again, who allows me to take that responsibility? The disciple! I am at the mercy of my disciples. Right now God is a vague idea for them, so today they may accept me and tomorrow they may leave me. On the outer plane the disciple may leave me; but as long as the Supreme wants me to concentrate on that person and send His Light to that person, I have to do it. After leaving our path, the disciple may not follow any path or he may go to some other path. But once I accept someone, unless and until the Supreme tells me that that person is in other hands, I am responsible for him.

I tell my students, "I am ready to take all your problems, provided you are ready to feel that you are for me and me alone. If your allegiance is scattered here and there, in this group and that group, and if you come to meditate at our Centre once in a blue moon, then even if you say that I am your Master, you have made me powerless to do anything for you. If you really give me your total existence, inner and outer, only then can I do something for you. It is on the strength of my absolute oneness with you and your total acceptance of me that I can take your problems."

When a Master of a very high order tells you that you have an eternal relationship with him, he is speaking on the strength of his absolute oneness with the Supreme and with your soul. He knows that you will always be under his inner guidance. And when you realise the Highest, you will see that the supreme Consciousness which you have realised is the same as the Consciousness that the Master represented on earth. A real spiritual Master embodies the infinite Consciousness of the Supreme and represents that Consciousness on earth.

When the Master speaks of an eternal relationship, this relationship is one of mutual acceptance. The Master does not say, "Whether you are aware of it or not, I shall keep my eternal connection with you and we shall be eternally one." No, if the Master really has the capacity to establish this eternal relationship with the disciple, then he also has the capacity to make the disciple feel that he has done it. The Master offers this message to the seeker's soul, and the seeker feels that his inner connection with his Master will last forever. Then with his utmost sweetness, concern, compassion, gratitude and pride, the Master accepts the disciple wholeheartedly and permanently. And the disciple will also have the same feeling for the Master; he will feel that the Master is not a separate entity but is his very own. He will feel that the very highest, which he calls the Master, is his own most illumined part. When he has that kind of feeling, that kind of realisation, then the eternal relationship between the Master and the disciple can dawn.

The eternal relationship between the Master and the disciple is significant only in the case of a realised Master. If the Master is not fully realised, then he is only fooling the disciple. There are many Masters who have not realised God but simply say, "Oh, we have an eternal connection. I will take care of you even after I leave the body." When this type of Master leaves the body, the disciple may cry to his Master constantly, but he will get no response. Even when he is on the physical plane, this type of Master can be of no use. He only makes false promises. The main purpose of initiation is to bring the soul to the fore. If there is no initiation, the purification of the body, vital, mind and heart can never be complete. If there is no initiation, then the highest Goal can never be realised. Those who are close to me have felt the actual flowering of their initiation the moment they have wholeheartedly dedicated to the Supreme in me their entire life—body, vital, mind, heart and soul. This flowering of the initiation is really more than initiation. It is the revelation of the disciples' own inner divinity. At that moment they feel that they and their Guru have totally become one. They feel that their Guru has no existence without them, and that they have no existence without their Guru. The Guru and the disciple mutually fulfil each other and feel that this fulfilment is coming directly from the Supreme. And the greatest secret the disciple learns from the Guru is this: that only by fulfilling the Supreme first can he fulfil the rest of the world.

How can the Guru fulfil the Supreme? The Guru plays his part by taking the ignorance, imperfection, obscurity, impurity and unwillingness from the disciple and carrying them faithfully and devotedly to the Supreme. The disciple fulfils the Supreme by constantly staying in the Guru's boat and in the inmost recesses of the Guru's heart, and by feeling that he exists only for the fulfilment of his Master. Him to fulfil, him to manifest: this is the only meaning, the only purpose, the only significance of the disciple's life.

*

The Guru is not the body. The Guru is the revelation and manifestation of a divine Power upon earth.

*

To meet God without an intermediary
May not be impossible,
But it is surely the loftiest
Mountain-climbing task.

*

Did you receive any help in learning the alphabet? Did you require a teacher to help you master your musical instrument? Were you given instruction to enable you to obtain your degree? If you needed a helper to do these things, do you not also require a teacher who can guide you to the knowledge of the Divine, the wisdom of the Infinite? That teacher is your Guru and no one else.

*

The Guru and the disciple must test each other sweetly, seriously and perfectly before their mutual acceptance. Otherwise, if they are wrong in their selection, the Guru will have to dance with failure and the disciple with perdition.

*

What does the acceptance of a disciple by a Guru
mean? It means that the Guru will gladly live in the
world of golden sacrifice.

*

The supreme initiation is when the Master says to
the disciple, "Take what I have," and the disciple says
to the Master, "Take me as I am."

# 2

# Choosing
# a Guru

A great teacher inspires
The seeker.

A great teacher aspires
In and through the seeker.

A great teacher knows
That he is the journey's soul
Of the seeker
And also his journey's goal.

## CHOOSING A GURU

There are three kinds of spiritual teachers. One will say, "I will do everything for you, my child. There is nothing for you to do. You may sleep, you may drink, you may enjoy vital life, you may do anything. You just remain in your own world and I will give you realisation and liberation. You don't have to do anything." You should remain thousands of miles away from that kind of spiritual Master.

The second type of teacher will say, "I have told you what the Truth is. I have tried to inspire you. I have played my part; now you have to work hard to reach your goal. Now you have to discover your own inner divinity." This kind of teacher does not solve any of the disciple's problems. This spiritual teacher is weak, even if he is sincere.

Then there is the third kind of teacher. On the strength of his absolute oneness with the highest Supreme, he says to the disciple, "My child, let us walk together. You shall aspire, and I shall bring down infinite Grace and Compassion from the Supreme. I have my own salvation, but I will walk with you and guide you. Let us work together." He is the real spiritual teacher.

How can an aspirant know if a Master professing to be realised is actually realised? A God-realised spiritual Master is not someone with wings and a halo to identify him. He is normal, except that in his inner life he has abundant Peace, Light and Bliss. So if you come to a spiritual Master expecting something other than boundless Peace, Light, Bliss and Power, then you will be disappointed. But again, you must know if you are fit to judge. If I know nothing about medical science, how am I going to judge a great doctor? Only another doctor will know how to judge him properly.

In the spiritual life, a real seeker who has sincere aspiration and dedication has already achieved a little bit of inner Light. Because of his aspiration, God has endowed him with an iota of Light, and with that Light he is bound to see and feel something in a true spiritual Master. If one is really advanced in the spiritual life and is making fast progress in his inner journey, then his aspiration will be the best judge as to whether a spiritual Master is genuine or not. The best judge is one's sincere aspiration.

An unrealised Master can fool you for a day or for a month or for a few years, but he cannot fool you forever. If your own sincere aspiration is one hundred percent pure and you want nothing but God, then God will not keep you with an insincere, unrealised Master indefinitely. It is impossible!

Very often people come and try to judge whether the Master is perfect or not. Here they can easily make a mistake. If the Master is genuine—that is to say, if the Master has realised God—then what may appear to them to be weaknesses in the Master will not hinder them in their self-realisation.

Again, so-called human weaknesses are one thing; but if the Master indulges in lower vital life, sex life, then that Master is very bad and you have to leave him. If you don't feel purity in the Master, if you don't see in him the perfection of the lower vital life, the emotional life, then you must give a wide berth to him. Otherwise, how will you ever get from him the perfection of your own vital life?

Some Masters do have their own realisation, true realisation, and still some of their disciples leave them. But do you think that a Master is not realised just because people have left him? No, it is the aspirants' own imperfections and limitations that take them away from their Master. Some people come up to a certain point and then their vital or ego comes forward and they don't want to go any farther.

After accepting the spiritual life for two years, six years, even ten years, some people become tired. If one becomes tired of walking on the spiritual path and leaves the path, it is not necessarily the Supreme's Plan. So don't try to judge a Master just because many are leaving him. Many will leave, but many others will come.

Even if a Master is genuine, he may not be meant for you. How do you know when you have found your own Master? It is like this. There may be many people around you, but when you see a particular person, immediately you get some joy. That means that your soul has some connection with that particular person. Ten persons may be right in front of you and for nine of them you may have no feeling. But one person's face or very presence gives you joy. In that case you have to know that this person has some inner connection with you.

If you have an inner connection with a genuine Master, it most likely has existed for many incarnations. So the moment you see that particular Master, you will get boundless, overwhelming joy. Your whole being will be surcharged with inner joy and light. You will feel that your life has at last found its source in the Master. You will feel that you are a leaf and the Master is the tree. The spiritual Master who gives you immediate joy, spontaneous joy, boundless joy, is your Master. Sometimes, if you are lucky enough, you may find your own Master the first time you see a spiritual Master. On the other hand, you may have to go to quite a few spiritual Masters.

When you find a Master whose very presence gives you immediate inspiration, joy, peace and delight, then you have to ask yourself the last and absolutely most important question: "If this Master does not give me realisation, liberation or anything that I want, am I still in a position to give him my love, my devotion, my surrender, my life?" If the answer is, "Yes, I don't want anything from him except to be allowed to serve him and give him what I have and what I am," then you will know for sure that he is your Master. He is absolutely your Master.

There is a saying, "When the student is ready, the teacher appears." But it happens many times, hundreds of times, that the Master has come and the disciple is also ready, but there is a veil of ignorance in front of the disciple. He is not seeing the light, although the light is right in front of him. If your own teacher stands in front of you and blesses you twenty times, even then you may not recognise him. The teacher recognises you, but he cannot tell you, "You are my student," for you will misunderstand. You will think, for example, "I have millions of dollars. That is why he is telling me I am his disciple. He is asking me to be his disciple just so that he can grab my money or this or that from me."

In this world, when we discover something for ourselves, then only do we feel that it is true. When somebody else discovers something and tells it to us, then we disbelieve, we doubt. If the realisation comes from within you that I am your Master, then you feel that it is your own discovery; but if I tell you, then you feel that you have every right to doubt me. I have seen quite a few sincere seekers who were destined to be my disciples and sooner or later did become my disciples; but something was preventing them from accepting me at the time. My telling them would not have expedited their recognition of me. On the contrary, this would only have delayed them further. So I remained silent in order that when the time was ripe they could have the satisfaction of their own discovery.

In the spiritual life, there are some teachers who can instruct you for a couple of years and there are some who can teach you right from the kindergarten level to the highest university courses. They have the capacity to take you up to the highest height. Even if a teacher is sincere, if he doesn't have the capacity to take you to the highest, naturally you will leave him when you have gone as far as he can take you. Again, there are so-called Masters who do not have the capacity to teach at all, but who will try to keep you as long as they can, just to exploit you. But it is you who have to know whether the teacher is able to help you. Your inner being will tell you whether you are making satisfactory progress or not. The moment you feel that you are not making any progress whatsoever in spite of your sincerity, then don't waste your time. You have every right to leave a teacher whenever you want to.

But what sometimes happens is that the teacher has true, genuine knowledge, but the student does not want to learn the truth in the way that the teacher wants to teach—or rather, in the way the Divine wants the teacher to teach. Very often, unfortunately, it happens that when a spiritual teacher tells the truth or unveils the truth, he is misunderstood by the doubtful mind of the aspirant. The aspirant asks a question, but his mental doubt does not allow him to accept the answer. Then, no matter how true, how significant and how sublime the answer may be, it is useless to the seeker.

Some seekers change their teacher almost every month. Today this teacher, tomorrow that teacher, the day after, somebody else. They are extremely rest-less and they will never attain illumination.

A teacher is like a boat. If you are in one boat, you are safe. But if you keep one leg in one boat and another leg in another boat, then you will just fall into the sea of ignorance. If you are securely seated in my boat or in someone else's boat, then the boatman is capable of taking you to the other shore. Then, once you reach your destination, you will see that all the boats arrived by different routes. The goal is one, but the paths are many. You cannot constantly change paths and hope to make the same speed. The seeker has to be wise, careful and discriminating.

Rome is one place, but there are many roads to reach that place, and each traveller will take a differ-ent road. Each Master is right in his own way. But once you choose a Master you have to stick to his path with total dedication and surrender. For you can only travel on one road at a time.

One Master teaches this, another Master teaches something else and a third Master teaches something completely different. You may feel it is like different subjects in school: history, geography, philosophy and so on. But I wish to say that in the spiritual life there is only one subject: God-realisation. For that one subject, the most profound subject, you should follow one particular path. If it is the path of devotion, wonderful. If it is the path of knowledge, wonderful. If it is the path of selfless service, wonderful. Again, you can combine all these into one. When you realise God, all paths become one; the three major paths of devotion, knowledge and selfless service inevitably merge into one.

We cannot say that our path is by far the best for everyone. Let us not be such fools. We can only say that our path is the path of love, devotion and sur-render. If others want to accept it, well and good.

Our path is the best for us and we are staying on this path because it is the path that the Supreme wants us to follow. Others also have to find the path that is best for them.

The spiritual path, the journey of the inner life, is a lifelong process. If you are ready to go through such a lengthy discipline, then only will you get your true Master. When you are studying you have to be serious in order to pass your examinations. Similarly, you have to be extremely serious and sincere in your spiritual life. So first please go deep within and feel whether you want a spiritual Master to guide you for the rest of your life and whether you can listen to him totally, wholeheartedly and unconditionally. If your feel that you can follow a Master faithfully and devotedly and give your life to his path, then the Master is bound to come to you. If you feel that you do not and cannot exist without the spiritual life, then you can rest assured that you are ready for the spiritual life. If you feel that you cannot stay on earth without inner peace, without inner joy, without the living guidance of God through a spiritual Master—if you have come to that stage—then you are bound to get a spiritual Master very soon.

There is no seeker on earth who will remain without a teacher if he is desperately in need of one. If his aspiration is intense, if his inner cry is constantly mounting, how can God remain asleep? It is God who has kindled the flame of aspiration in that particular seeker, and it is God who will bring a spiritual Master to him or place him at the feet of a spiritual Master.

*

There is a great difference between knowing the teacher and knowing his teachings. His teachings show the world what he has, but what he is, is another name for Eternity's Vision.

*

A seeker's struggling mind needs the right path.
A seeker's searching heart needs the right teacher.
A seeker's aspiring soul needs the right God.

*

Do not kill yourself worrying
    About false teachers.
Your sincerity-shield will protect you
And also definitely help you
    Find a real teacher.

*

    Only a false spiritual teacher
Thinks and feels
    That he alone is perfect,
And that the rest
Of the spiritual teachers
    Are all false.

*

Your Master does not hide from you.
It is your visionless eyes
And your restless mind
That do not allow you to recognise him
Even while he is standing
Right in front of you
With his Eternity's Compassion-Eye.

# 3

# The Realised Master

Not here but far away
Is the world of silence-peace.
Here and nowhere else
A God-realised soul shall bring
That world of silence-peace.

## THE REALISED MASTER

God-realisation is Self-discovery in the highest sense of the term — the conscious realisation of your oneness with God. As long as you remain in ignorance, you will feel that God is somebody else who has infinite Power whereas you are the feeblest person on earth. But the moment you realise God, you come to know that you and God are absolutely one in both the inner and the outer life. God-realisation means your identification with your own absolutely highest Self. When you can identify with your highest Self and remain in that consciousness forever, when you can reveal and manifest it at your own command, at that time you will know that you have realised God.

You have studied books on God and people have told you that God is in everybody. But you have not realised God in your conscious life. For you, this is all mental speculation. But when you are God-realised, you consciously know what God is, what He looks like, what He wills. When you achieve Self-realisation, you remain in God's Consciousness and speak to God face to face. You see God both in the finite and in the Infinite; you see God as both personal and impersonal. This is not mental hallucination or imagination; it is direct reality. This reality is more authentic than my seeing you right here in front of me. When one speaks to a human being, there is always a veil of ignorance — darkness, imperfection, misunderstanding. But between God and the inner being of one who has realised Him, there can be no ignorance, no veil. So you can speak to God more clearly, more intimately, more openly than to a human being.

It is inside the human that the divine exists. We do not have to live in the Himalayan caves to prove our divinity; this divinity we can bring forward in our normal day-to-day life. Unfortunately, we have come to feel that spirituality is abnormal because we see so few spiritual people in this world of ignorance. But real spirituality means the acceptance of life. First we have to accept life as it is, and then we have to try to divinise and transform the face of the world with our aspiration and our realisation.

People sometimes think that a realised person is totally different from an ordinary person and behaves in a very unusual way. But I wish to say that a realised person need not and should not behave abnormally. What has he realised? He has realised the ultimate Truth in God. And who is God? God is someone or something absolutely normal. When someone realises the Highest, it means he has inner Peace, Light and Bliss in infinite measure. It does not mean that his outer appearance or outer features will be any different. It does not mean that he will become abnormal in some way. No, he is normal. Even after a spiritual Master has realised the Highest, he still eats, talks and breathes just as others do.

Unspiritual people frequently think that a Master, if he is truly realised, has to perform miracles at every moment. But miracles and God-realisation do not necessarily go together. When you look at a spiritual Master, what you see is Peace, Light, Bliss and divine Power. Enter into him and you are bound to feel these things. But if you expect something else from a realised soul, if you come to a spiritual Master thinking that he will fulfil your teeming desires and make you a multi-millionaire, then you will be doomed to disappointment. If it is the Will of the

Supreme, the Master can easily bring down material prosperity in abundant measure and make someone a multi-millionaire overnight. But usually this is not the Will of the Supreme. The Will of the Supreme is for inner prosperity, not outer affluence.

A realised Master is like someone who knows how to climb up and down a tree very well. When the Master climbs down, he does not lose anything because he knows that at the next moment he will be able to climb up again. Suppose a child at the foot of the tree says, "Please give me a most delicious mango." Immediately the Master will bring one down and then he will climb up again. And if nobody else asks for a mango, he will sit on the branch and wait.

If you are fast asleep and someone pinches you and shouts, "Get up! Get up!" he is not doing you a favour. You will be annoyed. But the spiritual Master will not bother you; he will not ask you to get up. He will stay beside your bed and wait until you get up, and the moment you get up he will ask you to look at the sun.

Here on earth, if one human being has something to offer and the other person does not take it, then the first person gets furious. He says, "You fool! It is for your own good that I am giving it." He will scold the other person and be very displeased if his offering is not accepted. In the case of a spiritual Master, it is different. He will come with his wealth, but if humanity does not accept it, he will not curse humanity. Even if humanity insults him and speaks ill of him, he will not complain to God. With his boundless patience he will say, "All right, today you are sleeping. Perhaps tomorrow you will get up and see what I have to offer. I will wait for you."

A real spiritual Master will not lose anything if earth rejects what he has, because he is well established in his inner life and inner consciousness. Again,

if humanity accepts what he offers, he does not lose
anything, either. The more he gives, the more he gets
from the Source. This is not true of ordinary aspirants
or false Masters. If they give away something, they
cannot replace it. But the Master who is in touch with
unlimited capacity in the inner world has an infinite
ocean for his source. One cannot empty the infinite
inner ocean.

The real Master wants to give everything to his
devoted disciples, but their power of receptivity is
limited. So he tries to widen their vessels so they are
able to receive the Peace, Light and Bliss that he
brings. But he cannot force an aspirant to receive
more than the aspirant can hold. Otherwise, the
seeker's vessel will give way. A Master can only pour
and pour and pour his infinite Light into his disciples, but once the limit of their capacity is reached,
anything more that he gives will be wasted.

Some Masters are very selective and want only souls
that are fully dedicated, intensely aspiring and absolutely destined for the spiritual life. Sri Ramakrishna,
for example, wanted only a limited number of disciples and was very particular about whom he would
accept. But some Masters say, "Anyone who wants to
learn anything about the spiritual life is welcome to
my community. Then let everyone progress according
to his own standard." So they accept thousands of
disciples.

But no matter how many disciples they accept, if
they are true spiritual Masters they will only accept
disciples who are meant for them. If I know that
somebody will make faster progress through some
other Master, then occultly and spiritually I will make
that person feel in a few months' time that he is not
meant for me. What matters is not the number of
disciples a Master has but whether he takes them to
the Goal. If I am realised and somebody else is

realised, we are like two brothers with one common Father. Our goal is to take our younger brothers and sisters to the Father. The game will be complete only when all of humanity is taken to God. If two Masters are real brothers, then how can one be unhappy or displeased if somebody goes to their Father through the other? In the spiritual life, what matters is not who has done something but whether the thing has been done. Who has done it is only a question of name and form, which will be obliterated by history. What matters is that evolution has taken place on earth.

Again, you have to know that the true Master cares very deeply whether the disciples destined for him actually come to him. Sri Ramakrishna used to go up to the top floor of his house and cry for spiritual disciples. He used to ask Mother Kali why the disciples he was destined to have did not come to him. People may ask why he could not wait for God's Hour. In fact, God's Hour *had* come for Sri Ramakrishna, but the ignorance of the world was blocking it. God told him to do something and gave him the capacity, but ignorance was standing right in front of him and delaying, delaying, delaying his manifestation. Sri Ramakrishna was not crying for disciples who would come and touch his feet. He was crying for disciples who would be his real arms and hands, who would fly with him into the Universal Consciousness, who would work for him, and in that way, work for God.

Nobody is indispensable, true. But, at the same time, each person *is* indispensable as long as he is absolutely sincere in his aspiration and his service to the Mission of the Supreme. Out of pride and vanity nobody should feel that he is necessary; but everybody is necessary if he is a sincere, dedicated, chosen instrument of God. The Master needs disciples because they are the expression of his own consciousness. When he gets the Command from the Highest to do something on earth, then he has to try to find those who are going to be part and parcel of his consciousness to help him fulfil that Command.

Traditionally, spiritual Masters used to say, "If you have something, others are bound to come. The pond does not go to the thirsty person; the thirsty person comes to the pond." This is absolutely true if a mature person is thirsty. But if you feel that the thirsty person is just an infant, then it is all different. The baby will cry in his room, and the mother will have to come running to feed him. The mother does not say to the baby, "You have to come to me, since you want something from me." No, the mother puts everything aside and runs to the baby. In the spiritual world also, some Masters feel the need to go out into the world, for they feel the outer world is just a baby in its consciousness. These Masters feel that there are many children who are crying for spiritual life, spiritual wisdom, spiritual perfection, but who do not know where or how to find it. So the Masters go from place to place and offer their light with the idea of serving the divinity in humanity.

When the world is crying for inner food, if we have the capacity, we have to feed it. If I have the capacity to give you something and I also have the capacity to go and stand right in front of you, why do I have to call you to me? If I have the capacity both to place myself before you and to give you the spiritual nourishment that you want, then I must do so.

\*

A truly God-realised soul
Must cheerfully descend
Into the earthly human affairs.

*

He is not meditating
   For his own realisation.
That is already done!
He is meditating
   For your illumination.

*

A real Guru is the selfless, dedicated and eternal beggar who begs omnipotence and omnipresence from God to feed his unconsciously hungry and consciously aspiring disciples—in perfect conformity with their soul's needs.

*

The Guru is the spiritual magnet constantly pulling the disciple towards the infinite Light of the Supreme.

*

He alone is the divine leader who has the capacity to implant inspiration in the heart of the human soul.

*

A true spiritual Master must shoulder
The countless responsibilities
   Of his spiritual family.
But still he remains
In a childlike consciousness
To fill his seeker-children
With the joy and delight
   Of God the eternal Child.

# 4

# The Master and
# the Disciple

The seekers can make
The fastest progress
If they can dare to feel
That the Master's heart
    Sleeplessly cries for them
And the Master's soul
    Loves their lives
Infinitely, infinitely more
Than they can ever love
    Their own lives.

## THE MASTER AND THE DISCIPLE

A real spiritual Master is he who has inseparable oneness with the Highest. On the strength of this oneness, he can easily enter into the seeker, see his development and aspiration, and know everything about his inner and outer life. When the Master meditates in front of his disciples, he brings down Peace, Light and Bliss from Above and these enter into them. Then automatically they learn how to meditate from within. All real spiritual Masters teach meditation in silence. A genuine Master does not have to explain outwardly how to meditate or give you a specific form of meditation. He can simply meditate on you and his silent gaze will teach you how to meditate. Your soul will enter into his soul and bring the message, the knowledge of how to meditate, from his soul.

There are some who misunderstand the Master when he stands in front of them and prays. They think that, like themselves, he is also asking for Grace. They think, "Why bother the Master? Let us do it ourselves." But they don't realise that there is a vast difference between their prayer or invocation and the Master's. When the Master prays for Light, he becomes Light. When he brings down Grace, he becomes the fount of the Supreme's Grace. At that time, those who have faith in the Master get the all-nourishing and all-fulfilling Grace from Him.

Disciples who are in difficulty or who are suffering from illness often ask the Master to help them. Then, when the Master uses his spiritual power to cure them, they start praising their doctors or the wonderful medicine that they have been taking. The Master does not need their appreciation. If they want to say that he does not deserve it, then he is fully ready to agree. But their gratitude should go to the Supreme and not to the doctors or to some medicine. Again, sometimes people do feel the Grace that is brought down, but they think that *they* have brought it down on the strength of their own aspiration, or that they deserved it in some way or another. At that time the Master says nothing, waiting for the time when the seeker realises the truth himself. Inwardly he will convey the message to the seeker's soul, and after some time the soul will bring the message to the seeker's outer consciousness and the truth will be known.

The Master is like an ocean. When the disciple jumps into the ocean of the Master's consciousness, he is cleansed of all his impurities and immediately he will feel a temporary relief. You may ask, "Where do the impurities and imperfections go after entering into the Master?" The Master throws them into the Universal Consciousness. After a few minutes or an hour or some particular time, they are all gone from him. Sometimes the Master does not take them at all; he just offers them directly to the Supreme. The Master is blessing the disciple on behalf of the Supreme, as His direct representative, so he is not affected.

When the Master takes away the disciple's impurities, it does not mean that the disciple is cured of them. Tomorrow again the disciple will come back with the same impure thoughts and undivine ideas, because he is not conquering these unlit qualities within himself. Today he is sending his limitations into the Master, but tomorrow he will accumulate them again. So when the seeker offers his imperfections to the Master, he should try to receive as much Light as possible from the Master. If he can hold inside his inner vessel the Peace, Light and Bliss that the Master offers, then he will be able to fight against further imperfections in his life. Unless and until the disciple is able to retain the wealth he receives from the Master's blessings, he will not be able to achieve purity and make real inner progress—let alone realise the highest transcendental Truth.

A God-realised person can always be happy in his inner consciousness, where there is a constant flood of Light and Delight. The Master's unhappiness in the outer world comes from his disciples, because he identifies himself with all the wrong forces that they are suffering from. The Guru has the power to nullify the law of karma for his disciples, but while nullifying it he enters into their problems. If I have to pull someone out of the water, I have to be inside the water to help him. At the same time, I need conscious help from the one who is drowning. When the Master gets no cooperation from the disciples, when the disciples cherish their undivine qualities and will not let them go, then he suffers the most.

No disciple can ever make his Master happy if he or she is not happy inwardly. Even an ordinary human father will not be happy when he sees his daughter or son unhappy. Since the Master is a spiritual father, he can never be happy when his spiritual children are sad or depressed. If you cry because your husband is bad to you or because your wife is bad to you, the Master's compassion and sympathy are there. But if you don't throw the suffering off, then the Master's compassion is of no avail. If you cherish your depression and suffering, then the Master's help is useless. He will identify himself with your suffering and your heart's pangs, and he will suffer the pain that you are feeling—perhaps even to a greater extent than you yourself. But if you do not consciously try to rid yourself of the suffering and enter into the Master's illumined consciousness, then the Master's suffering and compassion will be futile. Also, you will not even be able to recognise it. You will not feel the Master's infinite compassion because you care more for your suffering than for your Master's divine love.

When you give your problems to your Master, you should not feel that you are overburdening him with a heavy load. The Master is ready to accept your ignorance. He has come here with the sea of Light; if you offer him the sea of ignorance, it will not harm him. But unfortunately, you feel that your ignorance is so precious that with one hand you give it and with the other you take it back. This moment you feel that ignorance is useless and you are happy to give it to the Master. You feel that you are very clever because you have given him something unimportant and have got something important from him in return. But the next moment ignorance makes you feel that what you gave him was much more precious than what he gave you; you feel that vital pleasure is much more important than Light. When you are in your deepest meditation, you feel that Light is more important than darkness. But when you are in the ordinary life, the life of desire, you feel that Light is all false and vague—all mental hallucination.

There are some disciples who get scoldings from their Master almost every day. Again, there are some disciples who do not get scoldings in the outer life even once in six months. But in the inner world the Master often scolds them and threatens them because he has taken complete responsibility for them. Often the teacher sees that the seeker's soul is more than eager to follow his guidance, but the vital hesitates and the minds resists. At that time, if the Supreme wants the seeker to fulfil his utmost potentiality and dive deep into the sea of aspiration, then the Supreme commands the Master to show his divine authority. True, when you live in the vital, you may think that the Master is scolding you; but when you live in the heart, you will see that it is his divine concern for you that is at work. And it is you who have given him the authority; he has not taken it. It is you, your heart, that has given him the authority to perfect you and mould you into the Highest, the Absolute.

There are two major ways that a disciple can eventually realise God with a Master. One way is to completely and consciously identify himself with the Master. Either you consciously identify with him and try to become one with him or you surrender to his will, which in a true Master is nothing other than the Will of the Supreme.

When you touch water, which represents consciousness, immediately the purity and soothing sensation of the water will enter into you. When you touch a flower, immediately you get the fragrance and purity of the flower. Just by touching you are identifying; and by identifying, you are getting the essence of the thing. Similarly, when you look at a picture of your Master in meditation, you are touching his consciousness. Then you identify yourself with him and become part and parcel of the infinite Consciousness that he has realised.

Again, through your conscious surrender to the Supreme in your Master, you become everything that he has and is. The tiny drop enters into the boundless ocean and becomes the ocean itself. This surrender is the surrender of your unillumined part to your highest part, which is represented by the Supreme in your spiritual Master. In this case, your Master represents your own highest self.

One day Sri Ramakrishna and two of his very close disciples were returning to their ashram in a boat. These two disciples and Sri Ramakrishna were extremely hungry. While they were in the boat, Sri Ramakrishna asked one of them to bring him some juice and food. When the disciple brought them, Ramakrishna did not give the others even a morsel. He ate and drank everything himself! But because of their identification with their Master, because of their oneness with him, these two disciples really felt that their hunger and thirst were appeased. They no longer felt hungry or thirsty at all.

If a disciple has established this kind of inner oneness with his Master, then he will not expect anything. The child does not expect things from his mother. He knows that his mother has given him and will continue to give him everything, for it is the mother's bounden duty to take care of the child. Similarly, it is your spiritual Master's bounden duty to be of constant service to you. You serve him with your aspiration and dedication; he serves you with his concern and compassion. You play your role with aspiration; this is your service. He plays his role with his concern and compassion, which uplift your consciousness; this is his service.

How can you play your role with aspiration? Early in the morning, when you leave your bed, you can say to the Supreme, "O Supreme, make me unconditionally devoted to You so that I can serve You in Your own Way." Then, before your breakfast you can repeat it again. As soon as you are through with your breakfast, say it once more. When you go to school or to work, you can again repeat it. Before performing any action, consciously pray that you will be able to serve the Supreme most devotedly and unconditionally.

Each time, the vibration of your prayer will last for two minutes, six minutes or ten minutes, depending on its soulful quality. But every time you offer this prayer you renew the vibration. Soon it will be like a bell. After you have started ringing the bell, it will become automatic and you will feel that the bell is ringing inside you constantly. Start offering your prayer early in the morning, and go on with it during the day. Each time you begin doing something, try to bring your devotion forward. Then, with each different activity, your devotion will grow.

An insincere disciple feels that the Master can be won by outer flattery. But the Master can be won only on the strength of the disciple's devotion to the Supreme in him and inner, conscious oneness with him. By telling the Master that he is great or by offering the Master material wealth, God-realisation cannot be attained. It is wonderful if you can dedicate your life, but real dedication has to be based on inner oneness. If the seeker wants the ultimate realisation of the highest Truth, the Divine in the Master has to be pleased in the way that the Divine wants to be pleased.

*

The human teacher says to the student,
"Work with me and I shall give you everything."
The divine Teacher says to the disciple,
"I have kept God waiting for you.
Don't delay; come with me to see Him."

*

He is an excellent spiritual Teacher
Whose eyes are firmness
And whose heart is forgiveness.

*

He can never be a real Master
If he accepts you as a disciple
    On your own terms.

*

It is not the spiritual Master,
    But the Supreme inside him,
Who deserves and receives
    The seeker's devotion.

*

Because he is God's representative
    Here on earth,
He is as careful with everybody's heart
    As he is with his own.

*

Love your Master.
It is the short way
    To spiritual progress.

Have faith in your Master.
It is the shorter way
    To spiritual progress.

Obey your Master.
It is the shortest way
    To spiritual progress.

*

There is no better way for a disciple to serve his
Guru than to listen to his advice.

# 5

# Oneness with the Master

His life is full of din,
His life is full of rush,
His life is full of hurry.
He is a picture of insincerity,
He is a picture of ingratitude,
He is a picture of failure.
He fails to silence the storm of his flesh,
He fails to come out of the abyss of his doubt,
He fails to bury the coffin of his fear.
   Yet
He shall be saved,
He shall be liberated,
He shall be fulfilled.
   For
He has heard his Master's footfalls.

## ONENESS WITH THE MASTER

Whether or not a disciple is outwardly close to the Master, the Master's heart-door is open to him twenty-four hours a day. If the disciple knocks at his Master's door, the Master will open it. But when he knocks, he must knock with his sincere aspiration and not with his demanding vital. If he comes with his demanding vital, the Master's door will never be open. But if he comes with aspiration, he will please the Master far beyond his imagination, and with just a faint knock the door will be open wide for him.

A disciple can please the Master in the Master's own way or in the disciple's own way. When the Master wants to be pleased in his own way, it does not mean that he is an autocrat. Rather, it means that the Master knows how the Supreme wants to be pleased. In the case of a genuine Master, the Master's will and the Supreme's Will are always one.

A disciple can best please his Master if he does not expect anything from the Master. He will only give and give; he will offer himself totally and unconditionally. Unfortunately, when the disciple gives something, often he immediately expects a specific thing in return. That is because he is living in the world of give and take. But the spiritual life is not a market. The Master knows what is best for the disciple and when is the best time to give that thing. If the Master gives something untimely, instead of illumining the unlit consciousness of the disciple, he may just break the disciple's inner vessel.

The power of the Master is bound to illumine the disciple if the disciple has receptivity. If the disciple has no receptivity, then the Master's power will be of no use. On the contrary, it will be harmful. But if the disciple allows the Master to operate in his own way, which is the way that the Divine commands, then the Supreme in the Master will be able to mould the disciple according to the divine Will.

There are four major ways in which disciples try to please the Supreme in their Master. First, there are some who want to please the Supreme in the Master in the way the Supreme wants to be pleased. How can they do that? On the strength of their aspiration and meditation they enter into the Master and get the message he wants to offer, and then they try to act accordingly. Or they let the Master enter into them and try to receive his messages. Every day the Master is communicating with the souls of his disciples, feeding them with Light, Peace and Bliss. Every day the Master is telling the souls how they can please the Supreme, and the souls are bringing the message to the disciples' conscious mind. Then the disciples either accept or reject the message.

Since, unfortunately, most disciples do not have the capacity to enter into the Master all the time or the receptivity to receive the Master's message, they try with all their sincerity, devotion and love to please the Master in the way that they feel is best. They may feel that if they do this for the Master, then the Master will be most pleased. It is a good attitude, no doubt, because they are trying most sincerely to please the Supreme in the Master — according to their capacity or according to the intensity of their aspiration. They are not trying to deceive the Master or create problems for him. They are only trying to serve the Supreme in him the way they feel best. The first way is far superior, infinitely superior; but even this second approach is also good.

Then there is a third way. Here the disciples feel that if the Master says to do something, they will do it; if the Master says not to do something, they will not do it. Then, if anything goes wrong, the poor Master has to take all the blame. But if things go right, immediately their ego comes forward and says, "It is our aspiration that was responsible for this success."

The spiritual Master says to these disciples, "If I say, 'Do this,' because that is the thing your own soul wants you to do, it is good that you do it. But if you would do it on the strength of your own inner feeling, then you would get infinitely more joy, because you would feel that you had discovered the truth your-self." The truth has already been discovered on their behalf by the Master. But now it is up to the disciples to discover in the inmost recesses of their own hearts that what they want and what their Master wants are the same thing.

The Master can tell the disciples, "Do this! Do that!" But he can say this only to those spiritual children of his who have totally offered to him their body, vital, mind, heart and soul — not to those who have just come to see whether he is a spiritual person and whether he can solve their problems. The Master has to do everything for those who have truly accepted him. But the disciples have to know that the Master is ready to serve them according to how deeply they have entered into him and how much they really love the Supreme in him.

A sincere disciple of any spiritual Master will always get the utmost joy by listening to the Master's dictates and not to his own physical mind. Those who are selfless, devoted and one-pointed walk along the Master's path every day, every hour, every second. If a seeker has this kind of devoted feeling for his spiritual Master, then he can make the fastest progress in his inner life.

Finally, there is a fourth attitude. Often so-called aspirants accept a Master for a day or two just so that he will solve their problems. Then, when their problems are solved, they go away. Or they say that they have come to the Master for liberation and realisation, but when they see that it is a long, arduous process, they leave him. They say that they have come for the highest realisation, but when they see that the Master's path is not the way that they want to realise God, they feel that the Master is not meant for them and they disappear.

Some people ask a spiritual Master what to do and when he tells them, they do exactly the reverse. If you know that you will not be able to listen to your Master, it is best not to ask him what to do. Otherwise, when sincerity enters into your heart and aspiration rises in you like a mounting flame, you will feel miserable that you did not listen to him. If you had not asked his advice in the first place, then you would not have felt miserable, because you would have had perfect freedom from beginning to end to make your own decision and execute it by yourself. When the Master gives advice, he is expressing the Will of the Supreme. It is up to the disciple to accept or reject it. If he rejects it, the Master will never be displeased. A real Master is far above the disciple's acceptance or rejection. But if the Master wants to, he can tell the disciple, "You are delaying your own progress. But God is inside you and He will continue to march. Slowly and steadily He will one day bring you to the Goal." More than that the Master has no need to say.

When the Master says something to a disciple, he is saying it for the disciple's own good. But unfortunately, very often when the Master speaks, the disciple thinks that the Master has some motive. Even if the disciple does not have that kind of feeling, he will often accept the Master's views with the greatest inner reluctance. What can the poor Master do? If he keeps silent, the disciple feels that the Master is indifferent to him. He says, "Master does not care for me; he cares only for others. He does not tell me anything." But even though the aspirant has been crying in the inner world for months or years for the Master's advice, when the Master tells him to do this or that, immediately the disciple objects. He tells the whole world, "Master has asked me to do this; that is why I am doing it. For myself, I don't want it or need it; I am doing it just to please the Master." In the inner world the disciples will cry for something; and in the outer world they will blame the Master for giving it to them.

A spiritual Master tries to please his disciples on all levels. At times he succeeds, at times he does not. At times he gets a hundred out of a hundred from them; sometimes he gets zero out of a hundred. He tries to please them most devotedly in the physical world, in the vital world, in the mental world, in the intuitive world and in the soul's world. Most of his disciples may not be aware of these inner worlds, but they are aware of the outer world in which they are living.

It is not always possible for the Master to please his disciples. Sometimes a disciple feels that the Master is unkind or does not care for him if the Master does not give him what he wants. But if the Master does give him what he wants, the disciple's soul will feel miserable and will curse the Master. And the Supreme will hold the Master responsible. He will say that the Master is consciously delaying the progress of that particular disciple. If a child wants to eat poison, the mother does not give him poison just to please him.

Each spiritual Master has three types of disciples: true disciples, false disciples and fanatical disciples. Fanatical disciples do not really believe what their Master says. They do not have implicit faith in their Master, but they want to make the world feel that they do. They insist that the entire world believe that whatever their Master says is the highest Gospel. But they don't have an iota of real faith in their Master. The fanatical disciples only want to show the world how much faith they have and how close they are to their Master.

False disciples feel that whenever they do something for the Master, they are doing him a great favour. They feel that the Master was drowning and they have brought him safely to shore. Although these people may have true sincerity and aspiration in their own way, they are not true disciples.

Those who find it difficult to accept the Master's judgement are also false disciples. They feel that truth has to be justified and mentally understood. If the Master says something to them, immediately they will ask, "Why? Why? Why?" They will always ask for justification. Unless and until their minds are convinced that what the Master has said is true or is coming from the Supreme, they will not do anything the Master requests. If the Master has to offer this kind of message repeatedly in order to convince the minds of some disciples, if he has to go on all his life justifying his conduct, then he can never do anything for these disciples. They are wasting their precious time and the Master is wasting his precious time. The mind can be convinced only for a fleeting second. The Master may take hours to convince the mind, but after a short time the same mind will again start doubting the Master.

Very often these disciples don't want real justification. They just want to show off their "tremendous wisdom." Or they feel that the questions they are asking have never been asked and that the questions themselves will remain immortal. But I wish to say that in this world all questions have already been asked and all questions have already been answered. When the disciple asks a question, he only changes a few words from a previously asked question. And when the Master answers the question, he also changes only a few words. Here on earth nothing is new. All the questions have been asked millions of times by millions of seekers; and all the answers also have been given by real spiritual Masters. It is nothing new; we are only using different phrases, different words, different idioms.

If the Master says something which you mentally do not understand, then meditate on it. You will come to understand the inner significance of the Master's statement. But by finding fault or demanding proper mental answers, you only satisfy your mental curiosity. At the same time, you literally pollute the pure hearts of those who either have established their oneness with the Master or want to establish their oneness with him. From the highest spiritual point of view, if the Master says that something is black, then his disciples will feel it is black even if it is white. Now you will say that black is black and white is white. But from the highest spiritual point of view, if a realised Master sees something as black and if you can enter into his consciousness and also see it as black, then at that time you will be establishing your inner oneness with the Master. And this is the beginning of God-realisation.

I tell my disciples, "If you feel that your way of seeing the truth is more powerful or more real, then I may agree with you in order to avoid complications. If I say, 'Do this,' and you say, 'No, no, that is wrong,' then immediately I will agree with you. I know that I am not wrong, but I don't want to argue. I will only wait for your soul to come forward and make you feel that I was right." Sometimes the disciples feel, "What does Guru know about this?" or, "What does he know about the outer life?" All right, then I will keep silent. But one day their souls will come forward and tell them that I said the right thing, absolutely the right thing.

In the spiritual life, at every moment we are aiming at the goal. While aiming at the goal, sometimes the football player pretends that he is going to kick the ball with his right foot. But if he feels that there is a very powerful opponent facing his right foot, immediately he changes the ball to his left foot and scores a goal. Now, just because it seemed that he was going to kick the ball with his right foot, immediately some people may think, "See, he could not score with the right foot; his right foot has no capacity. That is why he used his left foot." But what is ultimately important is scoring the goal. Whether one uses the right foot or the left foot to score is unimportant.

What is important is achieving the Goal and making you achieve the Goal. The true Master shall, without fail, take you to the Goal. But if the Master meets with greater opposition with a particular approach, then he will change it. You may be under the impression that he is making a mistake or that perhaps he did not see the truth. He sees the truth, but you have to know that he is dealing with possibility, and sometimes it is necessary to change his position.

True disciples are those who at every moment see the truth through the Master's eyes and feel the truth with the Master's heart. There is no sense of separativity between a true disciple and a real Master. Either the true disciples have already established their oneness with the Master on every plane of consciousness, from the highest to the lowest, or they are crying and trying to establish their inseparable oneness with the Master. They don't use the mind to judge whether the Master is right or wrong; they use the heart to become one with the Master's wisdom. If somebody feels the authenticity and reality of the Master's words, then he is bound to get the Master's consciousness. True disciples do not have to be told the reason why the Master says this or does that. They always feel that their Master is doing the right thing, and they know that he is doing it all for them. More than that, at every moment a true disciple is ready to fight with the Master against ignorance; and he will feel that the Master is fighting against ignorance not for the Master's own salvation but for the disciple's salvation.

To realise God is not like eating a banana or drinking a cup of tea. It is something really difficult! But the day you realise God, the Supreme, you will see that the price you have paid is too low. The price of God-realisation is never correct. Now the price is absolutely too high; there is not a single disciple who will say that the price is not high. But when you realise God, you will see that your Guru helped you to such an extent that the price was very, very low.

Each aspirant must consciously, soulfully, devotedly and unconditionally offer his will to the Will of the Supreme. When desire asks him to do one thing and aspiration asks him to do something else, he has to surrender the demanding vital and the doubting mind to the will of the aspiring heart and illumining soul. Sometimes the entire being wants to surrender all at once and jump into the sea of divine Reality, but the doubting mind says, "Be careful! Instead of a pearl, you may find some dangerous water animal." At this time, he must ignore the mind. When there is some hesitation on the part of the disciple, he is really lost.

In many cases, we know what the divine Will is, but we have not surrendered our own will due to lethargy or lack of intense aspiration. We feel that if we do not surrender this year, no harm; we will have many more opportunities before the end of our life. But if we cherish this kind of idea, then we will never surrender. When it is a matter of jealousy, insecurity or doubt, some disciples feel that if they cherish these forces today, tomorrow they will be able to conquer them at their sweet will. But that tomorrow will never come in their life. If you do not begin immediately, you will never begin and your nature's transformation will never take place.

You may say, "Previously I had more jealousy or more insecurity than now, so I am gradually making progress." But you have to compare yourself not with your obscure past but with your golden future. Feel that you are a divine warrior and you have to fight until the end. You may say that you have conquered 90 percent of your jealousy and only 10 percent remains. But I wish to say that until you have conquered the whole amount, there is no certainty of victory. Today you may feel that you have conquered some of these wrong forces; ten days later you will see that, like a wave, all the wrong forces have entered into your consciousness again and you are back where you started. Whenever you are aware of any wrong movement within you, please begin immediately to fight against it like a divine hero.

Again, some aspirants have the complacent feeling that they have walked a long distance and now they can take a little rest. But this is very dangerous. Even if you have only one step more to go in order to reach the ultimate Goal, you must not take rest. Even on the verge of realisation, many spiritual seekers have fallen. They have been swept away by temptation or doubt, and only after many, many years have they been able to resume their spiritual life. So you have always to be on the alert; you have to move forward continually.

No depression, no jealousy, no doubt, no fear can be allowed to remain inside you. If you retain undivine qualities, then you are digging your own grave. You cannot imagine what depression can do, what doubt can do, what jealousy can do! They can take you back to the animal life even though you are in a human body. They are doing it and they will continue doing it if you do not consciously throw them out of your life. If you really love the Supreme, then get rid of doubt, jealousy and all other undivine forces—completely and permanently.

Each aspirant has to make an inner promise to obey the Will of the Supreme—at least for just this one lifetime. He has to say to himself, "After all, this is only one life. Now I am 20 or 30 or 40 years old. I may stay on earth until I am about 80. Am I such a useless person that I cannot keep a promise or follow one course for a few fleeting years?" In your next incarnation, if you don't want to remain on the spiritual path, if you want to lead another kind of life, you can. But if you want to give the spiritual life a chance to please and fulfil you, you must live it in the proper way. Forget about Eternity and Infinity. Only concern yourself with one short lifetime out of the hundreds of lifetimes you have lived and you are going to live on earth. If you can really surrender your will to the Will of the Supreme for just one lifetime, absolute satisfaction will dawn in your life. Right now you are struggling and struggling to surrender your will to the Supreme. But I wish to say that each time you make this surrender you are gaining strength. Then, eventually you will reach the point where even if you want to have a will that is separate from the divine Will, you will not be able to, because you will have merged with

the one Will. At that point, yours will be the Victory
Supreme.

*

A pure heart
  Is imperishable.
A sure soul
  Is sovereign.
A true Master
  Is Infinity's Smile
    And
  Eternity's Cry.

*

Realisation can be achieved by God's Grace, the
Guru's grace and the seeker's aspiration. God's Grace
is the rain. The Guru's grace is the seed. The seeker's
aspiration is the act of cultivation. Lo, the bumper
crop is realisation!

*

Your Master is the sacred bridge
To help you cross the turbulent life-river
  And reach your destined goal.

*

If you sail in your Master's boat
  To the Supreme,
Then you and your Master will sing together
  Eternity's Oneness-Song.

*

A spiritual Master is a living dynamo
   Who at every moment
Inwardly and outwardly offers
Inspiration and aspiration
   In abundant measure.
The world has only to accept them.

*

You have a multitude of questions,
But there is only one answer:
The road is right in front of you,
And the guide is waiting for you.

# Stories and Plays

## THIS PLANT IS MAN,
## THIS PLANT IS GOD

There was once a seeker. For many years he had been looking for a Master, a Guru. Unfortunately he had not found one. He had been to many spiritual groups, but the teachers that he met were not to his taste. So he was still looking, looking for a spiritual Master. One day while he was walking along the street, he saw a spiritual Master with a few disciples. They were sitting on a lawn, a beautiful lawn, and some of the disciples were watering the grass.

This particular seeker approached the Master and said, "Master, all these disciples of yours listen to you no matter what you say. They believe in you and they are right when they listen to you. But I wish to say that I have something to tell you, even though you will not see eye to eye with me."

The Master said, "Truth is certainly not my sole monopoly. If you have discovered some truth, I will naturally accept your truth wholeheartedly. Now please tell me, what is the truth that you have discovered?"

So the seeker said, "My discovery is this: a worldly person cannot realise God so easily. I am a worldly human being, and I know that even to get a Master is simply impossible. I haven't found a spiritual teacher, for no spiritual teacher is satisfactory to me; so how will it be possible for me to realise God, which is infinitely more difficult? Just to get a Master is so difficult for me; to get realisation in this life is simply impossible. Do you agree with me?"

The Master replied, "Unfortunately, I do not agree with you. Others may think that what you say is right, but at this point I would like to say that it is not so difficult either to get a Master or to get God-realisation."

The seeker was surprised, and even the disciples were to some extent amazed at the Master's remark, because most of them knew how hard it had been for them to get a spiritual Master, and God-realisation was still a far cry.

The Master said, "Now look here. Right now some of my disciples are watering the grass. There are tiny plants around here." The Master pointed out two plants, two very tiny plants. Then the Master took a gardening tool and dug up one of the plants. Taking both the root and the leaf, the whole plant, he went to another plant. There also he dug up the whole plant and replaced it with the first one. Then he took the second plant and replaced it where the first one had been.

Then the Master said, "Look here. This plant is man, and that plant is God. Now I am the Master. I came here and I touched this plant. It was a matter of a few minutes, just a couple of minutes. As soon as I touched it, immediately the plant gave me the divine response, and I took it and put it there where the plant called 'God' had been. Then I took the God-plant and got all His Compassion, Love, Joy and Delight, and put it over there where man the plant was. It was a matter of only a few minutes. I took man to God and brought God to man."

The new seeker said, "Master, I wish to be your disciple. Please initiate me."

"I shall initiate you shortly, my child," the Master said. Then he continued, "If you feel that it is next to impossible to realise God, it means that your idea of God is wrong, your idea of spirituality is wrong. You are attached to the world, but if you had the same attachment towards God then you would see that you can easily reach God. Now when I go to God, I knock at the door. Immediately He opens it and comes to me. I say, 'Please come with me.' He comes with His infinite Love, Joy, Blessings and Compassion. Then I come and knock at your door, but when I knock at your door you don't open it. You keep your door closed, bolted. Naturally God and I go back. Then when I want to take you to God's Palace, I say to you, 'You come with me.' When I knock at God's door again, God says that as you didn't open your door when I brought Him to you, He will not open His door to you. If you had opened your door when I brought God as the Guest and if you had allowed God to come in, naturally God would also have allowed you to come into His Palace. So if you keep your heart's door open, God can easily come in.

"But when I approach you, immediately you are disturbed. You think that you have fear, you have doubt, you have emotional problems, you have vital problems, you have jealousy and so forth. You don't want to expose yourself; you want to hide. But this plant that I moved, man the plant, showed no fear, no doubt, no shyness when I touched it—absolutely nothing. It was not at all afraid of its own ignorance. It was thrilled that somebody was taking it to another place which was God. So when I touch you, when a spiritual Master blesses you or meditates on you, at that time if you offer your ignorance and your imperfections along with your devoted qualities, then it is so easy for the Master to take you totally to God. If not, it is next to impossible for the Master to do anything

to transform the consciousness of the disciples or even
to purify their consciousness. It is only an exchange of
two plants. This is what the Master does when he
deals with his spiritual children. One plant is God,
another plant is man."
Then the Master slowly walked away.

## THE MASTER'S ADVICE
## ON CHOOSING A PATH

There was once a spiritual Master who wanted to give each spiritual child of his special attention, concern, blessings and guidance, in spite of the fact that he had hundreds and hundreds of disciples. He conducted many meetings a week, sometimes two in one day, so that each meeting could be kept small and intimate, no matter how many new seekers he welcomed into his spiritual family.

On one or two days a week the Master allowed visitors to come and participate in the meetings, and some of them later decided to follow his path. One day four visitors—three boys and a girl—came up to the Master after a meeting. One of the boys bowed down to the Master and said, "Master, will you accept me as your disciple? I have been coming here each week for the last month, and I have finally decided that this is my path."

The Master asked the seeker his name and a few things about his outer life, and then in silence concentrated on his soul. Finally he said, "Certainly I shall accept you as my disciple. You have my wholehearted acceptance. Please come to our meetings regularly and devotedly. I can clearly see that this is your path."

The new disciple was extremely happy and grateful to be accepted by the Master.

Then one of the other two boys said, "Master, I too have been coming for the last month, but I have just found out that we can come only four or five times before we have to make up our minds about becoming a disciple. I feel that this may be my path, but I don't want to become a disciple right away since I wouldn't want to have any inner conflicts or be half-hearted in my commitment. I want to be absolutely sure."

The Master replied, "I deeply admire your sincerity. Unfortunately, we do have this rule here at the ashram, but you are most welcome to come to the meetings held on Wednesday nights outside the ashram instead. Many people have been coming to those meetings for eight or nine months or even a year, but they have not yet made a commitment and, on our part, we have not asked them to make any commitment. Of course, I am the same person, the same spiritual Master, whether I am in my ashram or outside it, so you will still have the same opportunity to decide if I am your Master."

"Master, I am happy to hear that I will be able to attend your Wednesday meetings, and I will certainly continue coming to meditate with you. But why do you have this rigid regulation to begin with? Forgive my asking, but why should one's inner life have these outer limitations?"

The Master explained, "My son, if we have some rules and regulations like this one, we can harmonise more effectively as a group. Every organisation needs rules and regulations so it can run smoothly. Also, it is easier to discipline the lives of the disciples in a spiritual community if there are some rules.

"There is also a spiritual reason, my son. I have seen clearly that if you want to select a path, four visits to one Master are more than enough for you to decide whether or not his path is the one for you.

After seeing me that many times, if I am supposed to be your Master, you are bound to feel something in me. I am not saying that just because I am a spiritual Master you have to feel something in me; but if I am meant to be your Master you will definitely feel something in me which will encourage and inspire you to become my disciple. If you say, however, that in your case it is taking more time because you want to be very careful and cautious to avoid making a mistake, then once again I would like to invite you to come indefinitely to that other meeting. Take your own time. After six months or so, if you feel that this is not the path for you, you can try other paths.

I am your older spiritual brother, let us say. Because I am a little more advanced than you in the spiritual life, my role is to take you to our common Father, but I myself am not the Goal. If there is somebody else who is also a little bit more spiritually advanced than you, then naturally he, too, will be in a position to take you to the Father. We spiritual Masters are like messenger boys; we just carry the seekers to the Father. You will have the same opportunity to realise God whether you accept this path or another path. If you want to take your time, then please do so, but don't feel sad or disturbed. At that meeting and at all my meetings—indeed, everywhere —my heart's door is wide open."

The second seeker bowed to the Master. "Master, I am deeply moved by your heart's magnanimity and your deep wisdom. I shall certainly continue to come to your meetings. Thank you."

Now the third boy approached the Master. "Master, I find that my life is in a state of confusion. How can I judge my own sincerity? Master, please give me some advice."

The Master said, "It seems to me that you have two questions, not one. One has to do with your confusion, another with your sincerity. Why are you confused? What makes you feel that you are confused? Acceptance of our path is one thing, but confusion in your own life, inside your own mind, is a totally different matter. Ask yourself if you will be happy if you do not accept our path. If you feel that you will be happy, and if you say that you are not confused in regard to rejecting or accepting our path, then your confusion is totally separate from whether or not you should accept the spiritual life. It is up to you either to accept us or reject us. This path is one way of seeing the truth. Your sincerity will tell you if it is for you."

"But Master," the seeker interrupted, "how can I judge my own sincerity?"

The Master replied, "You can easily judge your own sincerity. Your sincerity depends entirely upon your heart's wideness or magnanimity. You don't have to become a spiritual person in order to be sincere. Think of yourself as two persons. Think of your vital, mind and physical as someone drowning in the sea of ignorance, and think of your heart and soul as another person, swimming across the sea of ignorance. Separate your mind, vital and body from your heart and soul. Feel that while your mind, vital and body are drowning, your heart and soul have the capacity to save them. What should you do now? If you separate yourself from the drowning person, if you remain with the heart and soul, immediately the heart's wideness and the soul's vision of the future will come to save the drowning man inside you. But you have to decide whether or not you are willing to follow the path of the heart and the soul in order to save the physical, vital and mind. If you feel that the physical is giving you the right message, the vital is giving you the right message, the mind is giving you the right message, then you will not feel a real need for the spiritual life. But if you do feel that your mind, for example, is drowning, then you should turn to the heart, because the heart is in a position to offer illumination to the mind. When you enter into the spiritual life, your intellectual mind will be only an unfortunate obstacle. The mind, as such, is not bad, but the mind has to be illumined by the light of the heart. And the light of the heart comes from the soul itself."

The third seeker said, "Master, I will follow your advice, and I am sure thay my confusion problem and my sincerity problem will soon be solved. I will try to identify myself with my heart and soul."

Now the last visitor, the girl, said to the Master, "Although I have been meditating and leading an inner life for many years, this is the first time I have ever tried to find a Master. I feel a strong affinity with you, but is it too soon for me to make a decision?"

The Master said, "My daughter, enter into your heart and soul, and then if you feel that this is the path for you, certainly you should come here. If you feel that this is not your path, then go to some other place. But this is my only request to you and to everyone who has not accepted any spiritual Master: find your Master as soon as possible. Just because you are sincere, I am requesting you not to delay. You may say that you have to wait for God's Hour, but I say that the hour has already struck. That is why you have come here and you are thinking of going to some other places as well. Some people are very fussy. Although they see an object that they like in the first store they go to, they think that perhaps they will get something better in another shop. They go to twenty other shops, hoping to find a particular thing, and after looking and looking, they often end up coming back again to the first shop.

"But if people are wise, if they are really hungry
and they find the fruit that will satisfy their hunger in
the first shop, then they just eat it there and don't
bother going from store to store. Of course, if they
don't like the food offered there, they have every right
to go to some other place. But some people exercise
what they call human wisdom, which has no validity
from the spiritual point of view. Their very nature is
to say, 'Let us go and look at other things.' But the
difficulty is that time is very precious. If I have to look
around in many stores and browse through everything, while I am wasting my time somebody may
come and buy the fruit that I originally wanted. Also,
the shopkeeper does not keep his door open twenty-
four hours a day. If I browse in his shop for a long
time without buying the thing that I need, he may
decide that it is time for him to close his shop and ask
me to go look somewhere else. At that time, it is I
who will remain unsatisfied and unfulfilled.

"So, after going deep within, if your heart and soul
tell you this is not your path, be very brave and look
for some other Master. But if you feel that this is your
path, then don't allow the mind to come forward and
bring in doubts."

"You may think that the mind is being sincerely
cautious in questioning the heart, but the mind is
only showing its insecurity. The mind is helplessly
insecure, and that is why it always creates confusion.
Have faith only in your heart and soul. If the soul
conveys the message to you through your heart that
this is your path, accept this path and stick to it.

"What I am saying is that it is best always to be
alert and not to waste time. We have to study three
subjects. The first subject is God-realisation, the second
is God-revelation and the third is God-manifestation.
We have hardly even begun to study the first subject, but we have to complete all three courses.

Each course takes such a long time. God knows how many centuries, how many incarnations, each will take. So the sooner we start, the better for us."

The fourth seeker bowed and said, "Master, I shall not waste a second. I shall go deep within and find the path for me. Master, you are our true spiritual brother whose only concern is our progress. We are deeply moved by your unconditional guidance. We shall do what you have said." The four seekers bowed gratefully to the Master before leaving for home.

## I WANT ONLY ONE STUDENT: THE HEART

There was once a spiritual Master who had hundreds of followers and disciples. The Master often gave discourses at different places — churches, synagogues, temples, schools and universities. Wherever he was invited, and wherever his disciples made arrangements for him, he gave talks. He gave talks for children and for adults. He gave talks for university students and for housewives. Sometimes he gave talks before scholars and most advanced seekers. This went on for about twenty years.

Finally there came a time when the Master decided to discontinue his lectures. He told his disciples, "Enough! I have done this for many years. Now I shall not give any more talks. Only silence. I shall maintain silence."

For about ten years the Master did not give talks. He maintained silence in his ashram. He maintained silence everywhere. He had answered thousands of questions but now he did not even meditate before the public. After ten years his disciples begged him to resume his previous practice of giving talks, answering questions and holding public meditations. They all pleaded with him, and finally he consented.

Immediately the disciples made arrangements at many places. They put advertisements in the newspapers and put up posters everywhere to announce that their Master was going to give talks once again and hold high meditations for the public. The Master went to these places with some of his favourite disciples, who were most devoted and dedicated, and hundreds of people gathered together to listen to the Master and have their questions answered. But to everyone's wide surprise, the Master would not talk at all. From the beginning to the end of the meeting, for two hours, he would maintain silence.

Some of the seekers in the audiences were annoyed. They said that it was written in the newspaper and on the posters that the Master would give a short talk and answer questions as well as hold a meditation. "How is it that he did not speak at all?" they asked. "He is a liar," said many, and they got disgusted and left the meetings early. Others remained for the whole two hours with the hope that perhaps the Master would speak at the end, but he closed the meditations without saying anything. Some of the people in the audiences felt inner joy. Some stayed only because they were afraid that if they left early, others would think that they were not spiritual and that they could not meditate at all. So some left, some stayed with great reluctance, some stayed in order to prove themselves to others and very few stayed with utmost sincerity, devotion and inner cry.

It went on for three or four years this way. There were many who criticised the Master mercilessly and embarrassed the disciples, saying, "Your Master is a liar. How do you people justify putting an advertisement in the paper that your Master is going to give a talk, answer questions and hold meditation? He only holds meditation, and we don't learn anything from it. Who can meditate for two or three hours? He is fooling us, and he is fooling himself."

Some of the close disciples were very disturbed. They felt miserable that their Master was being insulted and criticised. They pleaded with their Master

again and again to give just a short talk and to answer
a few questions at the end of the meditation. The
Master finally agreed.

Now, on the next occasion, the Master did not
actually forget, but he changed his mind. He went on
meditating, and this time instead of two hours, he
conducted meditation for four hours. Even his close
disciples were sad. They could not get angry with the
Master, for it is a serious karmic mistake to get angry
with one's Master. But they were afraid that someone
from the audience would actually stand up and insult
the Master. In their minds they prepared themselves
to protect their Master in case some calamity took
place.

When four hours had passed and there was no sign
that the Master would either talk or close the meeting,
one of the very close disciples stood up and said,
"Master, please do not forget your promise."

The Master immediately said, "My promise. Yes, I
have made a promise to you people, so now it is my
bounden duty to give a talk. Today my talk will be
very short. I wish to say that I have given hundreds of
talks, thousands of talks. But who heard my talks?
Thousands of ears and thousands of eyes. My students
were the ears and the eyes of the audience — thousands and thousands of ears and eyes. But I have
failed to teach them anything. Now I want to have a
different type of student. My new students will be
hearts.

"I have offered messages at thousands of places.
These messages entered into one ear and passed out
through the other, all in the briefest possible moment. And people saw me giving talks and answering
questions. Just for a fleeting second their eyes glimpsed
something in me and then it was totally lost. While I
was speaking about sublime Truth, Peace, Light and
Bliss, the ears could not receive it because the ears

were already full of rumour, doubt, jealousy, insecurity and impurity which had accumulated over many years. The ears were totally polluted and did not receive my message. And the eyes did not receive my Truth, Peace, Light and Bliss because the eyes saw everything in their own way. When the human eyes see something beautiful, they immediately start comparing. They say, 'How is it that he is beautiful, his speech is beautiful, his questions and answers are beautiful? How is it that I cannot be the same?' And immediately jealousy enters. The human ear and the human eye both respond through jealousy. If the ear hears something good about somebody else, immediately jealousy enters. If the eye sees somebody else who is beautiful, immediately the person becomes jealous.

"The ears and the eyes have played their role. They have proved to be undivine students, and I could not teach them. Their progress has been most unsatisfactory. Now I want new students and I have new students. These students are the hearts, where oneness will grow—oneness with Truth, oneness with Light, oneness with inner beauty, oneness with what God has and what God is. It is the heart-student that has the capacity to identify itself with the Master's Wisdom, Light and Bliss. And when it identifies itself with the Master, it discovers its own reality: infinite Truth, Peace, Light and Bliss. The heart is the real listener; the heart is the real observer; the heart is the real student who becomes one with the Master, with the Master's realisation, with the Master's vision and with the Master's eternal Light. From now on, the heart will be my only student."

## HUMAN EXPECTATION
## AND DIVINE FULFILMENT

One day a close disciple of a great spiritual Master came to the Master and said, "Master, you have been telling me not to expect anything from my life, but to expect everything only from God. I do have faith in God, but unless and until I have seen Him face to face, how can I expect anything from Him? If I see a person, I may expect something from him, but if I don't see him, what can I expect from him? I see my hands, and I expect something from my hands. I see my limbs, and just because I see them, I feel that I can ask them for a favour. But in the case of God, since I do not see Him, how can I expect anything from Him?"

The Master said, "My child, it is true that you have not seen God, but I wish to tell you that there are many things that you get which do not actually come from an action of your hands, or eyes, or any part of your body. There are many things you don't expect, either from yourself or from anybody else, but these things do occur, even though you do not see any outer cause or any outer endeavour made by a person known to you. They come in God's own Way, which is far beyond your imagination."

"Master, that is true. But I must say that very often when I expect something from God, my expectations are not fulfilled."

The Master said, "When you expect something from yourself, do your expectations meet with fulfilment all the time?"

"No, Master."

"If you cannot satisfy all that you expect of yourself, why do you expect God to satisfy all that you expect of Him? Someone expects something because he has set a goal for himself, and he expects the goal to come and reach him or he wants to go and reach the goal. Because one has some destination in mind, either he pulls that destination into himself or he pushes himself to his destination. But one's own efforts are not always enough to give him success. No! There is a higher force, which is called Grace, the Compassion of God. When that Compassion descends from Above, there is nothing you cannot expect from your life. When divine Compassion descends, if you have a divine expectation, it is certain to be fulfilled.

"Again, in the beginning of his journey, a seeker may aim at a lower goal because he is not yet aware of his higher capacity, or because he is not freed from his desires. If the individual does not have real, sincere aspiration, if he is not a genuine seeker, then God will just give him what he consciously wants and expects. But if he prays and meditates soulfully, because God sees his sincerity and potentiality, God will not want him to reach the lesser goal. God is keeping an infinitely higher goal ready for him.

"In the beginning your expectation may be an iota of Light, but God is preparing you so that He can give you an infinite expanse of Light. In the beginning you may try to get just a drop of Nectar; you may feel that that is enough. But God wants to feed you a very large quantity of Nectar. So when you are totally sincere in your spiritual life, if you have a lesser goal, God may deny you your lesser goal because He has kept the highest Goal for you. But because you do not see the highest Goal, you feel that God is unkind to you and does not care for you."

"What is a lower or a lesser goal?" the disciple asked.

"Let me give you an example," replied the Master. "I used to want to become a ticket checker on a train. When I was a child and the ticket checker came by on the train and asked for the tickets, I was so fascinated by his movements and his gestures that I wanted to become just like him. Now, look! I have become a spiritual Master. To be a spiritual Master is an infinitely greater achievement than to be a ticket checker on a train. So God did not allow me to achieve this lesser goal.

"I also once wanted to become a great athlete, a very fast runner, but God wanted something else. He wanted me to become a very fast runner, not in the outer life, but in the inner life. The name, fame and achievement of the athlete who is a champion runner in the outer life last only for a few years. He inspires young people, true; but the inspiration he offers is nothing when compared with the inspiration that the inner champion, the spiritual Master, offers. When a Master inspires someone, that person's consciousness is elevated, and the person goes one step further toward the highest Goal. The ultimate Goal can eventually be reached with the help of a Master's inspiration and aspiration."

The disciple said, "But Master, even when I expect the highest Goal from God—Peace, Light and Bliss in infinite measure—even then my expectations are not fulfilled."

"My son, when you expect Peace, Light and Bliss from God, that means you have set yourself a very high goal. If you expect something from your friends, or your relatives, or your neighbours, or your acquaintances, if they don't want to give it, then they just won't do so. And as soon as you don't get it, you are unhappy because you feel that although you deserved it, you didn't get it; or you feel that others didn't want to give it to you because of their jealousy and fear that they wouldn't be able to show their supremacy if you got that thing.

"But in the case of God, if He does not give you something, it is not because He is jealous of you, or because He thinks that if He gives you His Infinity, then He will not be able to keep His Supremacy. No! You may feel that what you have received is only a tiny drop, while the thing that you are still expecting is an infinite ocean; but when God gives you only a drop, it is because He feels that even this tiny drop may be too much for you. But gradually God increases your capacity, and there will come a time when you will be able to receive a big drop. And finally you will be able to receive the ocean itself.

"If you expect something from God, but do not get it, rest assured that God has a very good and legitimate reason for not giving it to you. It is because He will give you something far better in the future. Also, He will tell you the reason why He is denying you. If He does not fulfil your expectation, He offers you Light. Through that Light, He makes it clear to you why He is not giving you what you expect. Again, if He gives you what you want immediately, then also He will tell you the reason you are getting it now. So, my child, if you really want to expect something, expect not from yourself, not from anybody else, but only from God.

"The fulfilment of expectation is at once a human necessity and a divine satisfaction. When we say we are satisfied, that is the fulfilment of our expectation. But this fulfilment of expectation takes place in a divine way only when we surrender our will to God's Will.

"Otherwise, we shall pray to God, meditate on God, worship God and try to please God with the wrong kind of expectation. Because we have prayed for eight hours, we shall expect God to give us a smile. But how do we know that by getting a smile from God our life will be immortalised, or that by getting something else that we wanted our life will be fulfilled?

"If we expect from God in a divine way, Reality will loom large in us; and, with this Reality, we will be able to go to our Immortality, our highest transcendental Goal."

## WHO IS MORE IMPORTANT —
## GURU OR GOD?

One day a spiritual Master happened to see a sad quarrel, a dispute between two of his disciples. The two disciples were almost fighting. So the Master approached them and said, "Now what is the matter? Why are you quarrelling and fighting?"

Both of them cried out, "Master, Master, help us! We need your guidance. We need your light."

The Master said, "If both of you speak at once, I cannot do any justice to you. So tell me, one of you, what is actually bothering you."

One of them said, "Master, the bone of contention is you and nobody else."

"What?" the Master said.

The disciple continued, "He says that the Master, the Guru, is more important than God. I say, impossible, God is more important. He says that the Guru is more important because the Guru shows the way, paves the way, and the Guru takes the disciple to God. He also says that although God cares for everyone, even the sleeping and the unaspiring, if one wants immediate concern and blessings from God, it is through the Guru that one can have it. That is why the Guru is more important.

"But I say, no, it is God who has given this kind of love and compassion to the Guru; it is God who has made the Guru an instrument to help mankind. So to me, God is more important.

"He says that there is a Goal, but if somebody doesn't take him to that Goal—that somebody being his Guru—then God will always remain a far cry. He says, 'The Goal may be there, but who is taking me to the Goal? I can't go alone; I don't know the road. So my Guru is more important, because the Goal will not come to me.'

"I say, no, the Goal may not come to me, but the Goal is God. Now if your Guru takes you to the Goal, God, and then God does not care for you, what is the importance of the messenger? The Guru can take someone near the Goal; but if the Goal doesn't care for that person, then naturally the journey is useless. A human being can take somebody to a Master, but if the Master is not pleased with the person he has brought, then the case is hopeless. The most important thing is not who has taken the disciple, but who is pleased with the disciple. If God is pleased with someone, then that is more than enough.

"He says that if the Guru accepts someone as his dearest disciple, then he takes on his shoulders the law of *karma*. When the father knows that his son has done something wrong and the father wants to save the son, he takes the punishment on himself. This is the Guru. But God is the Universal Father. He deals with His Cosmic Law. If we do something wrong, God will give us the consequences; we shall be punished. He feels that the Guru is more important, because the Guru takes on his own shoulders the punishment that the disciple deserves, whereas God will always follow His Cosmic Law.

"But I say, no, God is not punishing us; God is only giving us an experience. Who is punishing whom? God is having His own experience in us and through us. So we are not getting any punishment, but rather, God is enjoying or suffering through us, in us.

"Moreover, God existed before the Guru came into the field of manifestation, and God will continue to be God long after the Guru leaves the field of manifestation. The Guru came from God and he will return to God, his Source. But God is infinite and eternal. Never will He cease to exist. God is the All; the Guru is the temporary embodiment.

"Guru, I have the utmost devotion to you. Although he is saying that you are more important than God and I am saying that God is more important, I do have the utmost faith in you. Would you please illumine us in this matter?"

The Guru said, "Look, if you think that the Guru is the body, then the Guru is not at all important. If you think that the Guru is the soul, then Guru and God are equally important; they are one and the same. But if you feel that the Guru is the Infinite Self, the Transcendental Self, then you have to feel that it is neither the body of the Guru nor the soul of the Guru, but the Supreme in him, who is the Transcendental Self. The Supreme is the Guru, everybody's Guru. If you want to separate the physical, the soul and the Transcendental Self, if you want to separate them into three different parts, then you will never realise God, you will never be able to realise the highest Truth. In order to realise the highest Truth, you should serve the physical aspect of the Master, love the soul of the Master and adore the Transcendental Self of the Master. The most important thing is to see in the physical the boundless light of the Master; in the soul, the consciousness of inseparable oneness; and in the Self, the eternal liberation. Then only the Master and God can become one.

"God and the Guru are equally important in the Eternal Game, the Divine Drama."

# ONE MUST FOLLOW ONE'S OWN NATURE

(*A holy man is swimming in the river. An onlooker is sitting idly on the bank watching him. The holy man sees a scorpion right in front of him. Feeling sorry for the poor creature, he catches hold of it and very slowly, very gently puts it on land. While he is doing this, the scorpion stings him severely. The man begins to weep with pain.*)

HOLY MAN: I wanted to save you, and I did save you. Is this my reward? Anyway, I have done my duty.

(*A few minutes later the scorpion again falls into the river. Again the onlooker observes.*)

HOLY MAN: Ah, poor creature, you are suffering again. I feel sorry for you.

(*He lifts the scorpion again and puts it on land. Once more the scorpion stings him, this time even more severely. He screams with excruciating pain.*)

ONLOOKER: You are a fool! Why did you do that? The first time you made a mistake, and the second time you repeated the same mistake.

HOLY MAN: My friend, what can I do? My nature is to love, my nature is to save. The nature of the scorpion is to hate, the nature of the scorpion is to sting. I have to follow my own nature, and the scorpion has to follow its own nature. If it falls into the water again, I shall lift it up again, no matter how many times it falls. I shall be stung, I shall cry, I shall moan; but I shall not deny my nature, which is to love, to save and to protect others.

(*The onlooker immediately jumps into the river to touch the feet of the holy man.*)

ONLOOKER: You are my teacher, you are my Guru. I have been searching, longing for a Guru. Today I have found in you my real Guru. Since I am your disciple, from now on if the scorpion falls into the river it is I who will put it back on land.

(*Disciple sings.*)

*Amar bhabana*
*Amar kamana*
*Amar eshana*
*Amar sadhana*
*Tomar charane*
*Peyechhe ajike thai*
*Moher bandhan hiyar jatan*
*Timir jiban shaman shasan*
*Halo abasan nai nai ar nai*

[My thoughts, my desires, my aspiration,
   my life's disciplines
Have found their haven at Your Feet today.
The bondage of tempting attachment and
   pangs of the heart,
The life of darkness and the torture of death,
No more I see, no more I feel.]

*(He helps the holy man out of the river. The Guru now sits on the bank and watches the scene. In a few minutes the scorpion again falls into the river. The disciple catches hold of it and puts it on dry land, but the scorpion does not bite him.)*

DISCIPLE: How is it, Master, that I was not stung at all? I thought that I too would be stung by the scorpion. Twice you were stung mercilessly. I don't understand.

MASTER: My child, you don't understand? Shall I tell you? Will you believe me?

DISCIPLE: Please, please tell me. I shall believe you, Master.

MASTER: The scorpion also has a soul, and its soul told the scorpion that if it had bitten you, instead of putting it on land you would have killed it immediately. The scorpion knew that you would not accept it, that you would not tolerate its ingratitude. From you the scorpion did not get any assurance of its safety. The scorpion did not sting you because it felt this. In my case, the soul of the scorpion knew that I would never kill it, no matter how many times it might sting me; I would just catch it and put it on land for its safety. In the everyday world also people fight, quarrel and threaten others only when they see that their opponents are either weak or unwilling to fight. If they see that somebody is stronger than themselves, they will remain silent.

DISCIPLE: Master, do you have disciples?

MASTER: I have many, many disciples.

DISCIPLE: What do you do with them?

MASTER: I give and take, and take and give. I take their poison every day, and I give them nectar. I take their aspiration, and I give them realisation. I take from them what they have, ignorance, and I give them what I have, wisdom. They give me the assurance of my manifestation, and I give them the assurance of their realisation. We need each other. You need me so that you can empty yourself — your impurity, imperfection, obscurity and ignorance — into me. And I need you so that I can fill you with my all, with everything that is within me. This is how we fulfil each other. Your nature is to give me what you have: impurity, obscurity, imperfection, limitation, bondage and death. My nature is to give you what I have: purity, love, joy, light, bliss and perfection. When your nature enters into my nature and my nature enters into your nature, we both are totally manifested and totally fulfilled. This is how the seeker and the teacher fulfil the Eternal Pilot, the Supreme.

## TWO DISCIPLES

(*Two disciples in a room in their Master's ashram*)

FIRST DISCIPLE: I told you, I told you, I told you!

SECOND DISCIPLE: What did you tell me?

FIRST DISCIPLE: I told you that our Master has nothing. Nothing! He has no spiritual power. He has no occult power. He knows only how to talk. He talks about Transcendental Reality and Universal Consciousness and all about what he can do with his occult power. But it is all lies. He knows how to talk and we know how to listen to him. But he has nothing, nothing. Look, he has been suffering from his rheumatism for the last three months. If he had even an iota of occult power, he could have cured himself.

SECOND DISCIPLE: My heart tells me that he has the capacity to cure himself, but that God is asking him to have this experience.

FIRST DISCIPLE: He says he is taking on our *karma*, but we have done nothing. I have done nothing wrong. You and the other disciples have done nothing wrong. What happens is that he blames us when *he* does something wrong. Who knows what he has done wrong in the inner world? That's why he gets punishment. And outwardly he blames us.

SECOND DISCIPLE: He never blames us. And I believe him when he says he is taking our *karma*.

FIRST DISCIPLE: You believe him? Then believe him. Remain with him and suffer. Die with him.

SECOND DISCIPLE: I shall die with him. Not only shall I die with him, but I shall die for him.

FIRST DISCIPLE: God created two types of people on earth: one type to deceive, another type to be deceived; one type to be rogues, the other type to be taken advantage of.

(*Enter the Master. The first disciple begins to edge away. The second disciple touches the Master's feet.*)

MASTER (*to the first disciple*): So you know that I have no capacity, that I just brag? I am not the right Master for you. You will do the best thing by going to some other Master, or waiting for the right Master to come to you. Leave me. Go home and live peacefully. (*To the second disciple*) You believe in me. It is my duty to help you, to guide you. Now tell me, do you really feel that I take your ignorance, your imperfection into my body? Or do you just say it because you have studied my philosophy and books written by others? You have read about Ramakrishna, who took away the impurity, imperfection and ignorance of his disciples and suffered so much. Many, many spiritual Masters have said they have done the same. Do you think that I am just saying it because so many of them have said it? Do you think I am only talking, or do you think I actually take these things from you?

SECOND DISCIPLE: Master, I know what you take from me. Every day you take from me insincerity, obscurity, impurity, jealousy, doubt, insecurity and many other imperfections. Where do they go? I give them to you; they come to you. If there is nobody else on earth who believes it, I don't mind. Even if you tell me that you don't take it, that it is your own *karma*, I will not believe you. I know that God is giving you this experience for my sake. If I had gone through this particular experience, perhaps I would have died.

MASTER: My child, there are two reasons why I suffer. One reason is that I really take upon myself the burdens, the imperfections, the undivine qualities of my close disciples. That is what the Supreme wants me to do. There are two ways to take this *karma*. One way is to take it on oneself and suffer, and the other way is to throw the imperfections of the disciples into the Cosmic Consciousness. But the easier way, infinitely easier, it to take it on oneself. It is a direct way. You are suffering, and directly I touch you and take away your suffering. The other way is like carrying you to a different place, to the Universal Consciousness. The Cosmic Consciousness can be seen as a refuse heap. I take your impurities and imperfections and make them into a bundle. Then I have to carry that bundle there and throw it away. But the other way I just touch you and, like a magnet, I take away your sufferings, your pains, your undivine qualities. That way is easier and that's why I do it. God wants me to do this.

I say to God, "God, my children love me so much and I do not love them, I don't please them." Then God says to me, "Look how you suffer for them. Look at your own love, My son — how sincerely, how devotedly you love them. You feel that in your children's perfection is your perfection, which is absolutely true.

They love you just because they feel that if they can possess you, they will possess everything. They love you to have you; you love them so that you can bring them to Me. You love them because you feel that if you can bring them to Me, then you have played your part. By loving you for themselves, they feel that they have played their part. And when you love them, when you bring them to Me, to your Highest, then you feel that you have played your part."

Also, God has given me another reason to suffer. Many people come to me with only desire, desire, desire. They come to me only to fulfil their desires. But when they see that I am paralysed with pain, that I am also subject to suffering and disease, that I am as weak as they are, they say, "He is an invalid, he is helpless. How can he help us in any way? How is he better than us?" They feel the best thing is for them to go to somebody else who can help them, and many leave. But the truth of the matter is that God wants these people to leave me. When they leave, my boat becomes lighter and can then go much faster toward the Goal. God wants unaspiring people to leave their Master and make the Master's boat lighter.

So these are the reasons I suffer. When a sincere disciple sees that I am suffering for him, he says, "If I really love my Master, then I should give him only joy." So the disciple makes a promise, an inner promise: "I want him to be constantly proud of me. Nothing will give me greater joy than to see that my Master is always proud of me." So the disciple does not make any more mistakes and the Master becomes happy and proud.

(*The first disciple touches the Master's feet.*)

FIRST DISCIPLE: Master, for so long I was a faithless, inhuman creature. From today on I shall be your faithful, devoted disciple.

SECOND DISCIPLE: Master, I have been your devoted, faithful disciple for so long. Today you have told me the secret of your suffering. From today on I consider myself an important, conscious part of you. I consider myself an arm of yours. Master, your compassion is my life's only salvation.

FIRST DISCIPLE: Master, your forgiveness is my life's only salvation.

MASTER (*to the first disciple*): By recognising your stupidity, your ignorance, you have brought your divinity to the fore. (*To the second disciple*) By recognising me, my spiritual Truth, you have manifested God's Divinity on earth. You have manifested God's Will on earth.

# Our Path

# OUR PATH

*The following is a talk Sri Chinmoy gave describing his own spiritual path.*

Our path is basically the path of the heart and not the path of the mind. This does not mean that we are criticising the path of the mind. Far from it. We just feel that the path of the heart leads us faster towards our goal. Suppose I want to go to a place 300 miles away. I can reach my destination either by walking or by flying. Undoubtedly, I shall reach my destination considerably faster if I fly in a jet plane. Similarly, if we use the aspiring heart and not the doubting mind, we shall reach our goal much faster. The heart is all love. The mind is quite often all confusion. When we say the heart, we mean the spiritual heart, which is flooded with divine love.

The heart is strikingly significant because inside it is the living presence of the soul. True, the consciousness of the soul permeates the entire body, but the actual location of the soul is inside the heart. The soul has everything: Peace, Light and Bliss in infinite measure. We get these divine qualities inside the heart directly from the soul. And from the heart, we can bring them to the mind, to the vital and to the physical proper.

God is extremely simple. It is we who think of Him as someone complicated. God speaks the simplest language, only we don't understand Him. We are all deaf. We have been deaf for millennia. Poor God, He has been talking constantly, tirelessly, but we do not have time to listen to Him.

Our path is the path of simplicity. A child is simple; he loves his mother. He does not have to love anybody else; his mother is his whole world. He devotes himself to his mother. If his mother asks him to do something, he listens to his mother. A child is so simple that he tries to do everything to please his mother; and in pleasing his mother, he is doing the right thing and reaching his highest goal.

In the ordinary life, if someone loves another individual, then he spends most of his time with that particular person. He devotes his precious time to that person. If it is real human love—not divine love, but human love—then he sometimes surrenders to the other's whims even if they are absurd. He surrenders because the two of them have formed an inner and outer bond on the strength of their love. So if one loves another person, then one is ready even to sacrifice one's precious wisdom.

In the spiritual life it is totally different. Divine love never binds us. On the contrary, it expands us and liberates us. When we see and feel that we are being liberated, we feel inwardly a divine obligation to do something for our Inner Pilot. How can we remain aloof from the One who has given us everything, who has brought us the message of divine Love and Compassion? Will it be possible for us not to offer Him something in return? If we remain in the outer life, we only try to grab and possess everything, even what belongs to others. But if we live in the soul, we try to constantly give all that we have and all that we are to the Inner Pilot. Divine love means self-giving.

But just giving something, just offering something, is not enough. It has to be done with enthusiasm and an intense inner urge. We give to the Inner Pilot in ourselves and in others. While we are giving to someone else, we have to feel that we are giving to the divine in the other person, to the Supreme within him, who now needs this help from us. When we offer divine love to someone, we must do it gladly and soulfully. But while giving, we must not feel that we are doing the other person a great favour, that because we are in a position to help him, we are superior. No! We have to feel that God has given us a great opportunity to be of service to Him and we should be grateful to the person who has put us in a position to help or serve the Supreme in him. We have to feel grateful that we have become His chosen instruments when He could just as well have chosen others. We have to show constant gratitude for the very fact that He has employed us. This kind of devotion is our dedicated service.

Then comes surrender. This surrender is not the surrender of a slave to a master. An ordinary master will find fault with the slave, while feeling that he himself is always perfect. But in the case of the Supreme, it is not like that. When He deals with us, He feels that our imperfections are His imperfections. When he finds mistakes in our nature, He feels that these are all His mistakes. Unless and until we are perfect, God never feels that He is perfect. God is omniscient, omnipotent and omnipresent; it is true. But when it is a matter of perfection manifested on earth, God feels that He is still imperfect in me, in you, in everybody. The message of perfect perfection has not yet dawned on earth. We surrender to God wholeheartedly, knowing perfectly well that what we have is next to nothing and what we are is next to nothing. If we give our nothingness to Him, we become a chosen instrument of the Supreme and permit His Perfection to grow in us.

Love, fulfilment and God always go together. God will never be satisfied with something incomplete, unrealised, unfulfilled and unmanifested. He wants from us realisation, revelation, manifestation and perfection. If these things don't take place in this lifetime, then we shall have to take many more incarnations. But God will never allow anybody to remain unrealised and unfulfilled. Today it is time for you to realise God. Tomorrow it will be the time for your friend to realise God. The day after tomorrow it will be the time for somebody else to realise God. There is for each person an hour, which we call "God's chosen Hour." At God's chosen Hour a person is bound to realise God.

We feel that our path is easier and more effective in the sense that we don't have to read millions of books to know what the Truth is. We don't have to exercise our mind day in and day out to know what the Truth looks like. No! Truth is inside us, and it is crying to come to the fore. But unfortunately, we have kept the door shut and we are not allowing the Truth to come out.

Now how can we bring the Truth out of its prison cell? Again, I have to say it is through love. Love for whom? Love for God. And who is God? God is the highest illumined part in us. God is nothing and nobody else. I have a head and two feet. Let us say that my head represents the highest in me and my feet represent the lowest in me, my ignorance. I know that the highest and the lowest are both mine. The lowest has to enter into the highest in order to be transformed, liberated and fulfilled. The highest has to enter into the lowest in order to be revealed and manifested.

In our path, the sense of identification is absolutely necessary. The highest has to feel its total oneness with the lowest. The lowest has to feel its total oneness with the highest. Needless to say, the highest always feels its oneness with the lowest. It is the lowest that finds it extremely difficult to be one with the highest because of its fear, doubt, jealousy and so forth.

What kind of commitment is necessary to follow our path? It is not the kind of commitment that you have to make in other spiritual or cultural organisations. For these organisations, you may have to give a regular fee. But when I ask you to make a commitment, it is different. I say that if you see something in me, if you see or feel Light inside me, then if you want to follow our path, you can. There will be no monetary demands. You do not have to give me five dollars or ten dollars or anything like that. No! Here it is a matter of your own aspiration—how sincere and regular you can be in your spiritual life. If you are not sincere, then you will not be able to run fast. But if you are sincere and dedicated, then you will run very fast. The commitment I ask for in our path is regularity in your meditation and aspiration, a sincere inner cry. I ask nothing else from any disciple.

Our path, the path of the heart, is also the path of acceptance. We have to accept the world. If we enter into a Himalayan cave or sit on a mountain top and cry for our personal achievement and satisfaction, then we are not going to do anything for the world. It will be like this: I shall eat food to my heart's content and let my brothers remain unfed and starving. That is not good. If I am a real human being, I have to see that my brothers also eat along with me. If we eat together, then only we shall get real satisfaction.

Similarly, in the spiritual life, real spiritual Masters feel that it is their bounden duty to eat in front of humanity and share the spiritual food with humanity.

Now, if humanity as a whole does not want to eat as it should, if many are still sleeping and have not yet felt the spiritual hunger, then what can the spiritual Master do? But if there are a few sincerely hungry seekers, the spiritual Master tells them, "The meal is ready. Let us eat together."

In our path of acceptance, we have to know that the earth is far from perfection. But unless we accept the earth-consciousness, how are we going to perfect it? If someone has some pain, I have to massage him. Then only his pain will go. Similarly, if the earth is imperfect at a particular place, I have to touch it with my aspiration and concern. Then only can I transform it. As long as the earth-consciousness is not fully realised, I will try to remain on earth to be of service to mankind with my inner consciousness.

## ABOUT SRI CHINMOY

Sri Chinmoy is a fully realised spiritual Master dedicated to inspiring and serving those seeking a deeper meaning in life. Through his teaching of meditation, lectures and writings, and through his own life of dedicated service to humanity, he tries to show others how to find inner peace and fulfilment.

Born in Bengal in 1931, Sri Chinmoy entered an ashram (spiritual community) at the age of 12. His life of intense spiritual practice included meditating for up to 14 hours a day, together with writing poetry, essays and devotional songs, doing selfless service and practising athletics. While still in his early teens, he had many profound inner experiences and attained spiritual realisation. He remained in the ashram for 20 years, deepening and expanding his realisation, and in 1964 came to New York City to share his inner wealth with sincere seekers.

Today, Sri Chinmoy serves as a spiritual guide to disciples in some 80 centres around the world. He teaches the "Path of the Heart," which he feels is the simplest way to make rapid spiritual progress. By meditating on the spiritual heart, he teaches, the seeker can discover his own inner treasures of peace, joy, light and love. The role of a spiritual Master, according to Sri Chinmoy, is to help the seeker live so that these inner riches can illumine his life. Sri Chinmoy lovingly instructs his disciples in the inner life and elevates their consciousness not only beyond their expectation, but even beyond their imagination. In return he asks his students to meditate regularly and to try to nurture the inner qualities he brings to the fore in them.

Sri Chinmoy teaches that love is the most direct way for a seeker to approach the Supreme. When a child feels love for his father, it does not matter how great the father is in the world's eye; through his love the child feels only his oneness with his father and his father's possessions. This same approach, applied to the Supreme, permits the seeker to feel that the Supreme and His own Eternity, Infinity and Immortality are the seeker's own. This philosophy of love, Sri Chinmoy feels, expresses the deepest bond between man and God, who are aspects of the same unified consciousness. In the life-game, man fulfils himself in the Supreme by realising that God is man's own highest self. The Supreme reveals Himself through man, who serves as His instrument for world transformation and perfection.

Sri Chinmoy's path does not end with realisation. Once we realise the highest, it is still necessary to manifest this reality in the world around us. In Sri Chinmoy's words, "To climb up the mango tree is great, but it is not enough. We have to climb down again to distribute the mangoes and make the world aware of their significance. Until we do this, our role is not complete and God will not be satisfied or fulfilled."

In the traditional Indian fashion, Sri Chinmoy does not charge a fee for his spiritual guidance, nor does he charge for his frequent lectures, concerts or public meditations. His only fee, he says, is the seeker's sincere inner cry. Sri Chinmoy takes a personal interest in each of his students, and when he accepts a disciple, he takes full responsibility for that seeker's inner progress. In New York, Sri Chinmoy meditates in person with his disciples several times a week and offers a regular Wednesday evening meditation session for the general public. Students living outside New York see Sri Chinmoy during worldwide gatherings that take place three times a year, during visits to New York, or during the Master's frequent trips to their cities. They find that the inner bond between Master and disciple transcends physical separation.

As part of his selfless offering to humanity, Sri Chinmoy conducts peace meditations twice each week for ambassadors and staff at United Nations Headquarters in New York. He also conducts peace meditations for government officials at the United States Congress in Washington, D.C., and recently he was invited to inaugurate a regular series of meditations at the British Parliament.

In addition, Sri Chinmoy leads an active life, demonstrating most vividly that spirituality is not an escape from the world, but a means of transforming it. He has written more than 700 books, which include plays, poems, stories, essays, commentaries and answers to questions on spirituality. He has painted some 140,000 widely exhibited mystical paintings and composed more than 5,000 devotional songs.

Sri Chinmoy accepts students at all levels of development, from beginners to advanced seekers, and lovingly guides them inwardly and outwardly according to their individual needs. For further information, please write to:

Aum Publications
86-24 Parsons Blvd.
Jamaica, N.Y. 11432

## Additional Titles
## by Sri Chinmoy

### Meditation: Man-Perfection in God-Satisfaction

Presented with the simplicity and clarity that have become the hallmark of Sri Chinmoy's writings, this book is easily one of the most comprehensive guides to meditation available.

**Topics include:** Proven meditation techniques that anyone can learn • How to still the restless mind • Developing the power of concentration • Carrying peace with you always • Awakening the heart centre to discover the power of your soul • The significance of prayer. Plus a special section in which Sri Chinmoy answers questions on a wide range of experiences often encountered in meditation.
**$8.95**

### Beyond Within: A Philosophy for the Inner Life

*"How can I carry on the responsibilities of life and still grow inwardly to find spiritual fulfilment?"*

When your simple yearning to know the purpose of your life and feel the reality of God has you swimming against the tide, then the wisdom and guidance of a spiritual Master who has swum these waters is priceless. Sri Chinmoy offers profound insight into man's relationship with God, and sound advice on how to integrate the highest spiritual aspirations into daily life.

**Topics include:** The spiritual journey • The transformation and perfection of the body • The psyche • Meditation • The relationship between the mind and physical illness • Using the soul's will to conquer life's problems • How you can throw away guilt • Overcoming fear of failure • The purpose of pain and suffering • Becoming conscious of your own divine nature • The occult • and more.
**$10.95**

## Death and Reincarnation

This deeply moving book has brought consolation and understanding to countless people faced with the loss of a loved one or fear of their own mortality. Sri Chinmoy explains the secrets of death, the afterlife and reincarnation.
**$6.95**

## Kundalini: The Mother-Power

En route to his own spiritual realisation, Sri Chinmoy attained mastery over the Kundalini and occult powers. In this book he explains techniques for awakening the Kundalini and the *chakras*. He warns of the dangers and pitfalls to be avoided, and discusses some of the occult powers that come with the opening of the *chakras*.
**$5.95**

## Yoga and the Spiritual Life

Specifically tailored for Western readers, this book offers rare insight into the philosophy of Yoga and Eastern mysticism. It offers novices as well as advanced seekers a deep understanding of the spiritual side of life. Of particular interest is the section on the soul and the inner life.
**$5.95**

## The Summits of God-Life: Samadhi and Siddhi

*A genuine account of the world beyond time and space*

This is Sri Chinmoy's firsthand account of states of consciousness that only a handful of Masters have ever experienced. This is not a theoretical or philosophical book, but a vivid and detailed description of the farthest possibilities of human consciousness. *"Essential reading for all seekers longing to fulfil their own spiritual potential."*
**$5.95**

## Inner and Outer Peace

*"A powerful yet simple approach for establishing peace in your own life and the world."*

Sri Chinmoy speaks of the higher truths that energise the quest for world peace, giving contemporary expression to the relationship between our personal

search for inner peace and the world's search for outer peace. He reveals truths which lift the peace of the world above purely political and historical considerations, contributing his spiritual understanding and inspiration to the cause of world peace.
**$7.95**

## Eastern Light for the Western Mind
*Sri Chinmoy's University Talks*

In the summer of 1970, in the midst of the social and political upheavals that were sweeping college campuses, Sri Chinmoy embarked on a university lecture tour offering the message of peace and hope embodied in Eastern philosophy. Speaking in a state of deep meditation, he filled the audience with a peace and serenity many had never before experienced. They found his words, as a faculty member later put it, "to be living seeds of spirituality." These moments are faithfully captured in this beautiful volume of 42 talks.

**Topics include:** The inner voice • The quintessence of mysticism • The secret of inner peace • Attachment and detachment • Self-knowledge and self-control • The ego • How to please God • Fear of the inner life • God and myself • Individuality and personality • The body's reality and the soul's reality • Intuition.
**$6.95**

## A Child's Heart and a Child's Dreams
*Growing Up with Spiritual Wisdom—A Guide for Parents and Children*

Sri Chinmoy offers practical advice on a subject that is not only an idealist's dream but every concerned parent's lifeline: fostering your child's spiritual life, watching him or her grow up with a love of God and a heart of self-giving.

**Topics include:** Ensuring your child's spiritual growth • Education and spirituality—their meeting ground • Answers to children's questions about God • A simple guide to meditation and a special section of children's stories guaranteed to delight and inspire.
**$5.95**

**On Wings of Silver Dreams**
*The Spiritual Meaning of Dreams*
This collection of Sri Chinmoy's answers to questions on dreams guides us through the confusing labyrinth of the dream worlds, teaching us how to understand the significance of some common dreams, and also how to gain some control over the kinds of dreams we have.
**Topics include:** What are dreams • How to remember your dreams • Spiritual experiences received in dreams • What to do if you have a bad dream • Prophetic dreams • The meaning of colours in dreams • Dreams as a precursor of reality • and more.
**$5.95**

# Music of Sri Chinmoy

**Flute Music for Meditation**
While in a state of deep meditation Sri Chinmoy plays his haunting melodies on the echo-flute. Its rich and soothing tones will transport you to the highest realms of inner peace and harmony.
**(Cassette) $9.95**

**Inner and Outer Peace**
A tapestry of music, poetry and aphorisms on inner and outer peace. Sri Chinmoy's profoundly inspiring messages are woven into a calm and uplifting musical composition with the Master chanting and playing the flute, harmonium, esraj, cello, harpsichord and synthesizer.
**(Cassette) $9.95**

**Ecstasy's Trance: Esraj Music for Meditation**
The esraj, often described as a soothing combination of sitar and violin, is Sri Chinmoy's favourite instrument. With haunting intensity, he seems to draw the music from another dimension. The source of these compositions is the silent realm of the deepest and most sublime meditation.
**(Cassette) $9.95**

**Silence Speaks**

Sri Chinmoy plays the cello and flute. He also sings while accompanying himself on the cello and harmonium. This recording captures the intensity of Sri Chinmoy's unique style of devotional music. **(Cassette) $9.95**

**The Dance of Light: Sri Chinmoy Plays the Flute**

Forty-seven soft and gentle flute melodies that will carry you directly to the source of joy and beauty: your own aspiring heart. Be prepared to float deep, deep within on waves of music that "come from Heaven itself." Comes with a free booklet on music-meditation. **(Cassette) $9.95**

To order books or tapes, request a catalogue, or find out more about Sri Chinmoy or the Sri Chinmoy Centres worldwide, please write to:

**Aum Publications**
86-10 Parsons Blvd.
Jamaica, N.Y. 11432

When ordering a book or cassette, send check or money order made out to Aum Publications. Please add $3.00 postage for the first item and 50¢ for each additional item (maximum postage— $5.50).